IMAGES OF ENGLAND

BRIGHTON AND HOVE CINEMAS

IMAGES OF ENGLAND

BRIGHTON AND HOVE CINEMAS

ALLEN EYLES

TEMPUS

Frontispiece: The Duke of York's, Brighton, in 2003 (photographed by the author).

Front cover: The Regent, Brighton, in 1931 (courtesy of Chris Horlock).

First published 2003

Tempus Publishing Limited
The Mill, Brimscombe Port,
Stroud, Gloucestershire, GL5 2QG
www.tempus-publishing.com

British Library Cataloguing in Publication Data.
A catalogue record for this book is available from the British Library.

ISBN 0 7524 3069 6

Typesetting and origination by Tempus Publishing Limited.
Printed in Great Britain by Midway Colour Print, Wiltshire.

Contents

Acknowledgements

The history of Brighton's cinemas has been extensively researched before. This book is an attempt to explore the story in a little greater depth, bring it up to date, and present a wider range of illustrations.

My first debt is to John Montgomery and his weekly series 'Halls of Fame' in the *Brighton and Hove Gazette & Herald* in summer 1983. I have looked at D. Robert Elleray's *A Refuge from Reality: A History of Brighton's Cinemas* (1989, Olio Books, Hastings); Timothy Carder's *The Encyclopaedia of Brighton* (1990, East Sussex County Libraries); *Film-makers, Cinemas and Circuses at Hove* by Judy Middleton (2001); *Brighton: The Century in Photographs* Volumes I and II by Christopher Horlock (2000 and 2001, S. B. Publications) and parts of an unpublished (history *c.* 1990) of Brighton's cinemas and theatres by Ian Grundy and Bob Harris; and drawn on unpublished reminiscences by Dennis Williams. Two cinemas have been covered in great detail in *Picture House*, the magazine of the Cinema Theatre Association: John House's 'Regent Brighton' appeared in issue no. 10, Spring 1987, and my 'The Oldest Cinema? The Duke of York's Brighton' in no. 25, Autumn 2000.

I could not have undertaken this book without being able to draw on several photographic sources to supplement my own material. I am most grateful to: Chris Horlock, whose collection was simply indispensable, and who could not have been more helpful, even reading through the text; Tony Moss, the president of the Cinema Theatre Association, who opened up his huge pictorial archive; Keith Skone, my research collaborator on earlier studies of cinema history, for his notes and loan of images; Bruce Peter, fast as lightning with his contribution; and the ever-reliable John Fernee, who provided memories of Brighton cinemas, his own shots of several vanished interiors, and also combed the text. Sally Blann and her staff at the Local Studies Library of Brighton and Hove Libraries (now Brighton History Centre at the Brighton Museum) and Carrie Wiltshire (Assistant Curator - Toys, Media & Film) and Fran Stovold at Hove Museum & Art Gallery were of great assistance. The Cinema Theatre Association Archive, Step Back in Time (125 Queens Road, Brighton), Ian Grundy, Trevor Povey, Mike Storey and Bob Elliston were among other obliging sources of illustrations, with Judy Middleton a helpful intermediary, while Elain harwood and Richard Gray also assisted. In most instances, there has been no means of identifying the actual photographers.

I have not resolved all the problems relating to the history of Brighton's cinemas, especially in the early days, nor unearthed all the photographs I would have liked to find. I would be delighted to hear (c/o the publisher) from anyone with further information or photographs. If cinemas generally are of interest, consider joining the Cinema Theatre Association (website www.cinema-theatre.org.uk – or contact Membership Secretary, Flat One, 128 Gloucester Place, London W2 6HP).

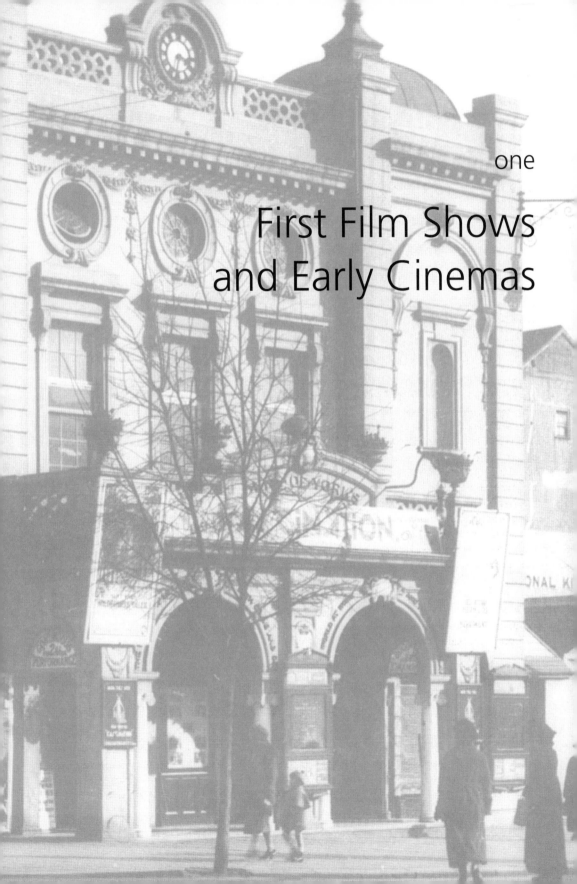

First Film Shows
and Early Cinemas

Public film exhibition began in Britain on 21 February 1896 with a programme of shorts made by the Lumière brothers in Paris using their Cinématographe, shown in central London. The Cinématographe's first appearance outside London was in Brighton a little over a month later. By Christmas, the Theatre Royal included a film item using the rival British Theatrograph system as part of its pantomime.

Although this book is concerned with permanent full-time cinemas, various venues presented occasional film shows, particularly in the period before full-time cinemas were established. They included the old Hove Town Hall, the Young Men's Institute in Holland Road, the Palace Pier Theatre, West Pier Theatre, the Aquarium, the Dome, the Hippodrome, and the Salvation Army's Congress Hall. In particular, the Hove Town Hall often presented travel or natural history lectures illustrated by film. The Hippodrome included films in its variety shows in 1905-1908 and presented special matinee shows of films of wild animals under the title The Cinema College. Some of these venues turned into cinemas. The Grand Concert Hall and Picture Palace, 78 West Street, Brighton, opened on Thursday 25 May 1911. First opened in 1892 as a long, narrow roller skating rink, it seated nearly 2,000 with a newly added balcony, and specialised in military band nights. Cinema use stopped in 1917, then resumed briefly from 1918 when it became the Coliseum Picture Theatre. The building found its true vocation as Sherry's Palais de Danse from 1919 to 1950.

Most of the early full-time cinemas are described on the following pages but some short-lived Brighton shop conversions have defied illustration: the Novelty Theatre, 27 West Street, opened in 1910, reopened in 1912 as the Empire Novelty Theatre, closed a few years later (the building was destroyed in widening the west side of West Street); the Imperial Theatre, 5 St James Street, known as the St James Cinema when it closed in 1916 (the building houses a charity shop in 2003; the extension at the back, visible along St James Place, was possibly added for cinema use); and the Royal Tierney Picture Theatre, 64 Edward Street, closed in 1914, reopened at the start of 1915 as the Picturedrome (or Picture Palace), renamed the Devonshire and then, from 1919, as the Majestic (Brighton Boys Club now occupies the site).

Some early cinemas which lasted are illustrated in a later period. However, images are lacking of the People's Picture Palace, 16 Lewes Road, a former stables turned garage used for film shows by touring exhibitors, first opened in the last half of 1910. It was reopened on Christmas Day 1911 following complete refurbishment, and needed further improvements in 1913. It had become the Arcadia by December 1913, the name under which it would survive until 1956. A subsidiary entrance, at the rear on Park Crescent, led straight into the auditorium.

During 1912, the Hove Cinematograph Theatre opened at 1 Western Road, on the corner of Little Western Street. Only just inside Hove, this cinema really belonged to the central Brighton scene. The 430-seat auditorium was a conversion by local architect Albert Carden of Jenner & Parker's auction hall, while the entrance took over Madame Ascot's dressmaking establishment. The cinema was run by a succession of proprietors, one of whom renamed it the Tivoli in 1916. It suffered from Hove's ban on Sunday film showings, only lifted in 1928 after a referendum.

In Brighton, cinema openings came to a halt in 1913 and the First World War prevented further construction. The cinema industry took a big step forward when feature-length productions were introduced, c. 1914. Subsequent cinemas needed bigger foyers, better toilet facilities and larger seating capacities because the shows were much longer.

THE CINEMATOGRAPHE AT THE PANDORA GALLERY

London's latest sensation, the Cinématographe, is now on view at the Pandora Gallery, King's road, opposite the West Pier. The first performances were given to-day, when the seances were attended by large and interested audiences. The description of the Cinématographe is somewhat of a difficulty, for its scope is as boundless as its results are marvellous. But according to the programme the cinematographe is the latest, and certainly it is the most astonishing development of instantaneous photography it has ever been our lot to witness. On an endless transparent band, we are informed, a series of "snap shot" photographs are taken at the unprecedented speed of 900 per minute, these being reproduced in an enlarged form by the cinematographe on a screen at the same astonishing speed at which they have been taken. The result, as may be gathered, is indeed marvellous, and every subject that was introduced at the seance it was our fortune to be present at to-day was reproduced with wonderful fidelity of movement and minuteness of detail. There were nine subjects reproduced and all were indeed so marvellously true to nature that one was almost led to imagine that the pictures contained real living figures instead of their being photographs only. The "Burlesque Highland Reel" was excellent, and "Red Indians preparing for the Warpath" was also splendidly reproduced, the photographs depicting the various movements and facial expressions of the figures being most realistic. "A Skirt Dance" in which the graceful flow of the skirts were reproduced to the life, and "Two Rounds of a Glove Contest" proved also exceedingly interesting. So true to nature are the photos that in "A Cock Fight" one could even see the feathers flying out of the fighting birds. The cinematographe is certainly what it claims to be—one of the sensations of the century. We can strongly recommend our readers to visit this wonderful show, and we are confident they will be satisfied with the result of their visit. Seances are given daily from 11.30 a.m.

Advertisement and report from the *Sussex Evening Times*, Wednesday 25 March 1896, for the first film show in Brighton, starting that day, at 132 Kings Road. The opening had been postponed from the preceding Monday. Advertising continued until Saturday 11 April when it referred to the 'Cinematographe or Vitascope' and 'New subjects added for the holidays. Enormous success of *Trilby*, Svengali's death scene to the life.'

From 1 July 1896, the Pandora Gallery was renamed the Victoria Hall to show films using R.W. Paul's system, the Theatrograph or Animatographe. Paul's half-hour show, which included a forty second record of the Derby, ran until 8 October, presented continuously on an 8ft. by 6ft. screen for eleven hours a day, audiences paying sixpence for entry. This was Brighton's first cinema (films returned here in the mid-1950s).

The site is now occupied by the Melrose restaurant. As part of the Centenary of Cinema celebrations, a plaque was unveiled exactly 100 years after the first film show by Joan Morgan, aged ninety-one, the star of many silent films made at Shoreham. Sadly, corrosion from the sea air has made the wording almost illegible: 'On this site stood The Pandora Gallery where films were first shown to the public outside London 25th March 1896.'

Opposite above: The Queen's Electric Theatre, 129b-130a Western Road, in 1910 (from Keith Skone's collection). Starting out as the Electric Theatre on 13 January 1907, it occupied just half the frontage seen opposite, as a shop conversion to the plans of architect Herbert A. Finn for the owner, W. Harold Speer, a former Fleet Street journalist, who also hand-cranked the projector. It had space for around fifty people and was so successful that Speer acquired the adjoining shop. He then had architect Thomas Garratt add an extension at the back of the two properties to contain the front stalls, orchestra pit and proscenium arch. Two identical entrances were created at street level. The upper front part of the two properties was rebuilt to provide a balcony, but the structural wall between the two shops had to be retained, and divided the rear stalls and circle with archways cut through to allow patrons to cross from one side to the other. The wall reduced the number of seats as it obstructed sightlines. While this unique adaptation took place, the original cinema remained open until the last three days, after which the enlarged premises were relaunched on the Saturday afternoon of 30 July 1910 as the Queen's Electric Theatre.

In the photograph opposite, the prices of admission marked above the doors range from threepence to four times as much, one shilling. A cosy corner (or box) in the balcony seats four, bookable in advance. Notices promise 'No Waiting', 'Continuous Performances' and 'Come In When You Like'. The words 'Electric Bioscope' were reinforced at night by small light bulbs. Lines of almost invisible bulbs also outlined the main name sign.

Continuous ninety-minute shows changed on Wednesdays and Saturdays and patrons could buy a book of twenty seats for the balcony for just over half the normal price. It now seated 250 with upstairs seating in tiers, and the performances of short films (varied to offer 'Mirth', 'Mystery', 'Comedy' and 'Drama' etc.) were accompanied by a trio of musicians called The Queen's Orchestra.

At the time of its 1910 reopening, Mr Speer showed his audiences a short version of *Faust* accompanied by the Animatophone, an early attempt to synchronise songs and music with the images. Two weeks later the *Brighton Herald* reported: 'In spite of its enlarged size, it proves yet too small to hold its patrons. Arrangements have been made to alter parts of the balcony lounge, raising it above the seats, and thus making more room for seating accommodation.'

Pathe's Animated Gazette was 'Shown regularly every Week immediately it is Published.' In addition, like many early cinemas, the Queen's made its own newsreel of local events which were developed locally and put up on screen later the same day. Mr Speer went on to produce fiction films, some of which were shown at the cinema.

Shortly after the photograph was taken, windows above the name sign were boarded over, with circular openings emphasised by light bulbs.

In one early publicity stunt, the Queen's exhibited a 'merman', the male equivalent of mermaid. In the summer of 1912, posters announced that the temperature inside did not exceed 62°F thanks to 'real ice breezes from the flower-decked ice grotto.' The trade paper *The Bioscope* was moved to note: 'The running of the projector is practically inaudible, as the windows of the operating-box are covered with glass.'

Eddie Scriven has recalled: 'The air was sprayed with a perfumed antiseptic from time to time during the performance by an attendant with a kind of syringe.' This practice became widespread, to counter the impression of cinemas being breeding grounds for various diseases.

Left: The first large Brighton cinema, seating 1,250, was a former music hall in New Road, almost adjacent to the larger Theatre Royal. This had been rebuilt in 1891 as the Empire Theatre of Varieties, to the plans of Charles E. Clayton of Clayton & Black, who later designed the Duke of York's cinema (1910) and the West Pier Concert Hall (1916). Films were shown as part of the bill by the turn of the century. It was renamed the Coliseum, *c.* 1902. When it was acquired by Tom Barrasford, who ran the town's Hippodrome, he turned it over to his wife, Maude, to relaunch as the Court Picture House in 1909 since there were too many theatres in Brighton. Minor artistes performed in support of the films. In this view, *c.* 1910-11 (courtesy of Step Back in Time), the arches are outlined by light bulbs and the words 'Court Theatre' have been crudely added to hide the Coliseum name higher up. Mrs Barrasford sold the Court to a London concern in 1918.

Above: The Theatre de Luxe, 150 North Street, Brighton, opened *c.* spring 1910. The cinema's rather discreet entrance can be seen to the right, in around 1920, advertising *On the Quiet* and *The Miracle of Love*, as a procession in honour of Earl Haig passes by. Cinemas had become big business by 1910 and this 500-seater was opened by Electric Theatres (1908) Ltd, a London-based company operating the Theatre de Luxe cinemas at Birmingham, Gloucester, Norwich and Plymouth, and in London at Camden Town and Ealing, along with other cinemas. (Photograph: Chris Horlock).

The conversion of the former *Brighton Gazette* printing works was by London architect Melville S. Ward, one of the first specialists in cinema work. The entrance was behind three arches illuminated by 200 electric lamps after dark. A huge sign on the top of the building used green-hued mercury vapour electric lamps to draw attention to its rather modest entrance. *The Bioscope* (7 April 1910) notes: 'The interior of the hall is decorated in the fifteenth century style, with oak beams and rough-cast panelling and roof, red-shaded electric lamps supplying partial illumination. The floor of the body of the hall slopes gradually downwards from back to front, whilst on the right-hand side is a spacious lounge and promenade, the latter feature being an innovation in picture theatre design.'

Advertising in 1911 refers to hour-long shows changed Mondays and Thursdays. Typically, adult prices ranged from threepence to one shilling for 'lounge seats'. In 1912, films were interspersed with songs by popular vocalists, and John Cher reported in *The Bioscope* (8 August): 'As I passed through the brilliantly lighted white entrance hall into the theatre, artistically decorated in the style of the Tudor period, and was conducted to my seat by a smartly uniformed attendant, Pathé's *Judgment of Solomon* was being screened. This fine picture play in Pathecolor, accompanied by appropriate music played on a piano and organ, was attentively watched by the audience and at the finish received loud applause.' By February 1915, a daily edition of the Pathé Gazette provided the latest war news, but the cinema was refused a licence for 1917 until its ventilation system was improved, and seems to have reopened on 31 January. By 1927 it had become the Cinema de Luxe, 'Brighton's "Bijou" Picture House'.

Below: The Electric or Gem, 36a London Road, *c.* 1912. Opened by July 1910, this very modest cinema served its immediate area. It was a converted shop that seated about sixty on wooden benches but claimed a capacity of 200. It charged only twopence and threepence admission. Nevertheless, the members of staff, including an imposing commissionaire, pose with pride for this photograph (from Chris Horlock's collection). The programme of short films is advertised on handwritten strips that overfill the display case in the centre. A row of light bulbs above draws attention at night. The two doors to the right serve as the entrance with the ticket window on that side of the central pay box, the doors on the left being perhaps the only exit. Operated by Eddie Scriven for his father Harry from 1913, it closed in 1915 or 1916 and has subsequently reverted to shop use. In 2003 its site is part of a branch of the Woolwich Building Society.

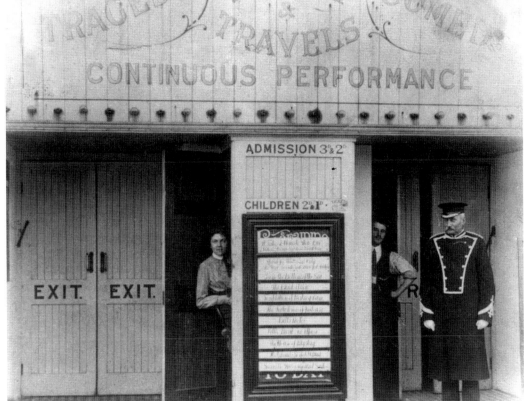

The Duke of York's at Preston Circus, Brighton, opened on 22 September 1910 and is still going strong in 2003. The early picture on the left seems to date from the afternoon of its opening, to judge from the absence of advertising, the bunting, and the unfinished look of the shop on the right. The rare view below (unearthed by Chris Horlock) dates from November 1912 and shows a full house, seemingly mostly children, with people standing at the back of the stalls. The box shown on the left remains to this day, though opened up. The view opposite shows the Duke of York's around 1922, with St Bartholomew's church in the hazy distance. Note the way that advertising has sprouted over the lower façade.

The Duke of York's was an adaptation of part of the malthouse of Longhurst's Brewery, previously the Amber Ale Brewery. The impressive frontage was entirely new as the original front of the building, further forward, was demolished in 1901 to make room for tramlines to curve past. The rear part of the malthouse was saved and adapted to become the cinema auditorium. The architects, Clayton & Black, created the elliptically curved ceiling that survives to this day. The balcony (supported by columns), proscenium arch and stage all had to be designed and built. The decorative scheme was in red and cream.

Tip-up seating for 800 people included two boxes, one at each side of the balcony, priced at two shillings and sixpence. An American pipe organ and an electric piano accompanied the silent films. The carpet was Wilton, there was air conditioning by electric fan that cleared the air in three minutes, and it had the largest projection room in Brighton, operated by electricity. Shows were originally two hours in length. Its long-lasting slogan claimed: 'Bring Her to the Duke's - it is fit for a Duchess.' There was an inscription in stone (no longer evident) which read: 'The mirror of life both grave and gay/The world at work the world at play.'

It was named the Duke of York's Theatre after the West End live theatre with which its first proprietor, Mrs Melnotte-Wyatt, was associated. She sold the Brighton Duke of York's to one Jack Channon in 1918.

Among early memories collected from patrons by manager Mike Vickers in the 1970s are the noise of the projector, as there was no glass in the portholes and it made a clicking noise that could be heard whenever there was a join in the film; and the spirited rendering before every performance of 'God Bless the Prince of Wales', demanded of the audience by the manager who conducted them from the orchestra pit, the reason being that the Prince of Wales at the time was also the Duke of York.

Regarding itself as one of the town's leading cinemas in the silent period, the Duke of York's took prominent newspaper ads decorated with catchy remarks. When the Regent had *Way Down East*, the Duke of York's advert commented: 'Way Down East or Way Up West, The Duke of York's Is Always Best'; and when showing *The Sign on the Door*, it added: 'The Sign On Our Door: Welcome' etc.

Opposite page: The Empire Picture Theatre in Haddington Street, Hove, opened on 10 December 1910. It is seen (above) in late 1911/1912 (courtesy of Tony Moss), and (below) *c.* 1915 (courtesy of Step Back in Time). Hove's first cinema was a conversion of Blatchington Hall, on the corner of Blatchington Road and Haddington Street, to plans by Bostel Brothers for Harry Scriven. The first projector came from the Salvation Army Congress Hall in Union Street. The cinema's entrance was at the south end of the building down the side street, to take advantage of the existing layout of stage and gallery (balcony). The small foyer occupied the back left hand corner of the stalls floor, creating an awkward shape of auditorium. The curtains helping to keep daylight out of the stalls can just be seen on the left in the lower picture, as can the staircase on the right to the gallery. The name sign calling it 'The First Hove Empire' is a reference to the Empire that quickly followed in George Street. In the days before feature-length films there were two shows nightly with a list of the shorts being shown. The original capacity has been put at 225 with the first four rows made up of wooden benches, the rest being velvet-upholstered tip-up seats with arms. A new balcony added seventy more places from 1912. While Scriven's son Eddie worked as a projectionist there in the early years, he also filmed local scenes for showing in the cinema.

Below: Portslade gained its first cinema when the Prince's Imperial Picture Palace and Theatre opened on Wednesday 15 March 1911 in North Street, on the site of the old Salvation Army citadel. It is seen here on the left, at the corner of Albion Street. Operated by (Mrs?) H. Gutteridge (or Guttridge), it had a modest capacity of 450. This was renamed the Picturedrome after it was taken over by Sussex Picturedromes around 1918. Its seating capacity was then stated to be 350, but it had only 298 seats by the early 1930s. (Photograph: Step Back in Time.)

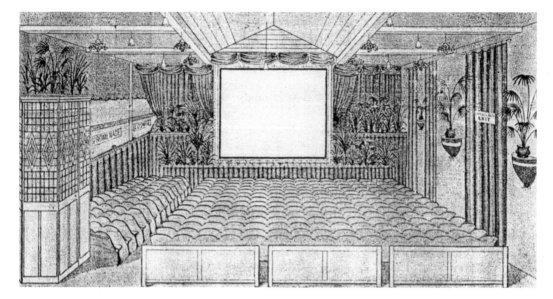

The Bijou Empire, 64 North Street, Brighton, *c.* 1911, in a drawing from the collection of Keith Skone. One of Brighton's most central and enduring cinemas began life around April 1911 as the Bijou Empire, or Bijou Electric Empire, as it was often called. It was a conversion of the Southern Publishing printing works, with an entrance between 62 and 63a North Street, although it was numbered 64. A piano and organ accompanied the films.

The Bioscope reported on 23 October 1913 that 'extensive alterations have been in progress for some considerable time.' The architects were the local firm of Brickwell & Bullock. The following month, there was a party wall dispute when Mr Griffin, a local florist, sued the cinema for alleged trespass and sought an injunction.

In any case, the cinema reopened as the Select Palace on the afternoon of Monday 8 December 1913. *The Bioscope* observed: 'Entrance to the theatre is obtained by means of an arcade, with a handsome mosaic pavement, and brilliantly lighted. An important feature in the decoration of the interior consists of a number of plaques bearing seascapes, which adorn the walls... Some £8,000 has been spent upon the building, which seats about 650.' *The Argus* (9 December 1913) noted that the auditorium sloped, rich curtains veiled the entrances, and that small lamps were placed under alternate steps in the balcony. Prices were sixpence, ninepence and one shilling, and the shows, which changed on Mondays and Thursdays, were continuous from 2.30 p.m. to 10.30 p.m.

A *Bioscope* report the following month added: 'The brilliant vestibule with its white and gold decorations and lavish use of electric light adds very materially to the brightness of North Street and tempts many passers-by to sample the excellent fare.'

In February 1914 it came under the control of George Bloch, who also operated the Coronation and Imperial. Another period of closure for building work occurred in 1915 when a fireproof wall was constructed (quite where is not clear: between the projection room and the auditorium?), after which it reopened as the Princes, the name it would retain for the next fifty years.

Hove's second Empire, the Electric Empire Picture Palace, at 76-77a George Street, opened on 11 April 1911, just five months after the one in Haddington Street. Being purpose-built and up-to-date (to plans by West Midlands architects J.H. Hickton and H.E. Farmer), this was far superior to its rival. It had an excellent position halfway down a busy shopping street and its temple-like exterior (above) stood out with its two domed pavilions like those at the Duke of York's. Inside (below) there were 350 seats on a single floor. A further Hove cinema, a Palmeira Picture Palace on Holland Road, was proposed in 1913 but never materialised. (Photographs: Step Back in Time (above); Tony Moss Collection (below).)

On Saturday 3 June 1911, the Academy Picture Palace opened at 59 West Street, Brighton. This former Turkish Baths retained an Oriental look inside and out, with marble-paved vestibule and handsome exterior (the steam cellars remained, disused, under the stalls floor). An enterprise of H.T. Underwood and E.E. (Teddy) Lyons (who lived in Brighton), it became part of their Biocolor Picture Theatres circuit. The Academy signed up for Kinemacolor, a real two-colour process (not colour tinting of black and white film), devised by Brighton inventor G.A. Smith and marketed by Charles Urban, who licensed the exclusive rights to one particular cinema in an area, supplying films in Kinemacolor along with the special projector needed and a qualified operator. By 1911 every part of the country had been licensed and this may have encouraged William Speer to launch the rival Biocolour in Brighton that year. Kinemacolor lasted until 1914.

The Academy originally seated 900, had its own occasional newsreel (or topical, as they were known in 1912) showing beauty parades, royal visitors etc., and engaged a full orchestra. After closing for enlargement, it reopened on 27 September 1913, claiming to seat 2,000 in comfortable upholstered seats. In November 1913 it made a big fuss about having *Hamlet* with Sir Johnston Forbes-Robertson, and the following month it presented one of the first feature-length films, the Italian epic *Quo Vadis?*. An extensive vestibule with staircases and gallery leading to the circle was entirely open to the street until being largely enclosed by a wood and glass screen in time for Christmas 1913. Films could be shown from any part of the world (with English titles inserted) and a Japanese picture called *The Wrath of the Gods* was a big success at the start of 1915.

Opened in 1911, the Coronation in North Road, Brighton (named after the coronation of George V that year) had a 350-seat auditorium which extended behind shops at right angles to the entrance, with exits onto Cheltenham Grove. On 20 November 1913 it reopened with the addition of a balcony to raise seating capacity to 550. Its proprietor, George Bloch, also owned the Imperial and later the Bijou Empire. In June 1922 the cinema was relaunched as the New Coronation. By the end of 1933, it had become the Troxy.

Left: This is the façade of the Coronation as it is being recreated in 2003 by Brighton architect Miles Broe, based on original drawings. The old foyer will become his practice's offices. The auditorium has already been demolished and replaced by flats.

Overleaf: The Palladium, on the Brighton seafront on Kings Road as a cinema, *c.* 1918. This was the former Alhambra variety theatre, opened in 1888 and designed by Frank Matcham (who was also responsible for Brighton's Grand Theatre and Hippodrome, the latter surviving in 2003 on Mecca bingo). The Palladium is advertising the British film *The Elder Miss Blossom*. It made up for its narrow frontage with a striking canopy and by its towering height. A very long foyer led to an auditorium which went straight back, widening out to the right. At the end of the alley where the back wall can be seen, posters are on display. There was a separate pit or front stalls entrance on Russell Street (to the other side of the shop to the left).

After going over to films, the Palladium had changed its name to Grand Cinema de Luxe by April 1912 but reverted back from 15 February 1913 under new management. A *Bioscope* report of 23 October 1913 notes that it had shown a topical film of great local interest, *The Boy Scouts Farm at Wadhurst*. With its large capacity of nearly 2,000, it was able to bid for some of the biggest attractions of the day, and in November 1915 it collared the Italian epic *Cabiria*. Eddie Scriven recalled packed houses for D.W. Griffith's spectacular *The Birth of a Nation*, with a full orchestra of ladies (men being at war). It seems to have advertised itself as both the Palladium and the Palladium Opera House for several years, settling on the former by 1919. It continued as a cinema until 1956.

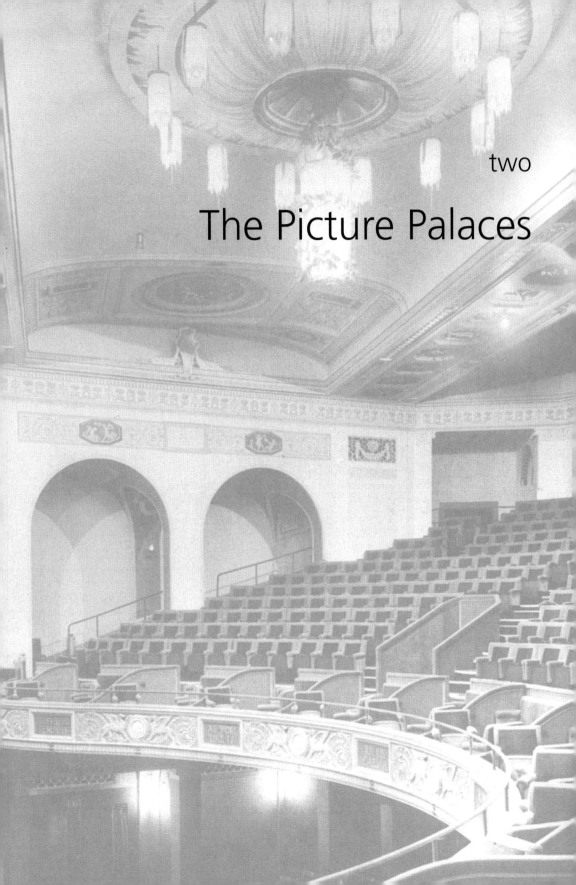

two

The Picture Palaces

In 1921 Brighton welcomed the Regent – the town's most impressive cinema, at least until it was severely damaged by fire in 1929 and the original proscenium arch was replaced rather than restored. The other newcomer of the 1920s was the tiny King's Cliff, a converted chapel that brought cinema to Kemp Town at the start of the decade. No further cinemas opened in the 1920s. A major scheme for a Stoll Cinema costing £500,000 in West Street was abandoned in April 1929 (the site was eventually used for the S.S. Brighton).

The only cinema to close in the 1920s was the one in Edward Street, detailed earlier. Others changed their names, usually on the back of some improvements and/or a change of ownership. In 1922, the proprietor of the Tivoli, George Beyfus, acquired and refurbished the Queen's Electric on the other side of Western Road, reopening it as the Scala.

A major development was the creation of two companies that would combine making and distributing films with building a national circuit of cinemas. The Gaumont-British Picture Corporation acquired its very first cinemas, the Biocolor circuit, from E.E. Lyons and Thomas Underwood on 18 November 1926. These included the Academy, Brighton. In May 1928 Gaumont took over the General Theatre Corporation, which ran both the Court Theatre (with attached billiard room) and the Hippodrome at Brighton. However, the new combine's biggest coup was its acquisition of Provincial Cinematograph Theatres, the leading national chain with ninety-six cinemas that included the Regent, Brighton. The deal was completed in February 1929, just after the fire at the Regent. Although Gaumont happily retained the Academy as a second house, it disposed of the Court as being surplus to requirements.

For cinemas generally, the major change was the arrival of talking pictures from 1929 onwards. During the 1930s, three big cinemas opened in the centre of Brighton, and two in Hove. The Savoy, Brighton, was a true rival to the Regent with its lavish decor, huge seating capacity, ability to obtain major new releases, and its cafés, restaurant and dance floor.

When the new and fast-expanding Odeon circuit arrived in West Street, Brighton, its theatre ranked with the Regent and Savoy as one of the area's Big Three – indeed, these were the key cinemas in Sussex, the first in a very wide area to show the weekly new releases of the three national circuits.

The Astoria, Brighton, was another large cinema, but was soon run as a secondary house by ABC, playing the best of the leftovers until it came into its own with extended runs from the late 1950s. The Gaiety was a suburban hall, boldly streamlined both inside and out – certainly the purest expression of 1930s Moderne among the town's cinemas.

In Hove, the Lido (a conversion of a skating rink) and the Granada were both substantial newcomers that knocked out the two small early cinemas, and had access to major new films, especially once they became part of the Odeon and ABC chains respectively.

There were other newcomers, as illustrated on the following pages. And several older cinemas were modernised. The Scala/Regal in Western Road, and the Academy in West Street were transformed into very up to date cinemas, externally and internally (the former taking a new name, the Curzon). Others changed their facades and smartened up the foyer, but did little with the auditorium. One cinema almost left it too late to make any improvements: the Kingscliff at Kemp Town reopened on Saturday 2 September 1939, the day before war was declared. Because of the threat of conflict, not all of the materials had been delivered and the refurbishment was incomplete.

The main entrance of the Regent, Brighton, at 138 Queen's Road, by the clock tower, as it looked after opening in 1921 (courtesy of Chris Horlock). Note the slope of the road, the cinema's name discreetly confined to each end of the canopy, and the battery of lights on top of the canopy to illuminate the frontage at night. The promoters, Provincial Cinematograph Theatres (PCT), had bought the site in 1914. After the First World War, the cinema's architect Robert Atkinson went to the United States to study the latest developments in movie theatre design. The resulting £500,000 scheme originally added an underground ballroom, a winter garden on the roof and a restaurant and café. The first signs announcing the venture went up in January 1920. However, excavating the site proved hugely expensive and slow, because the slope of the land opposed the rake of the stalls floor, and local residents successfully objected to work at night. PCT asked Atkinson to revise his plans, and the ballroom was relocated to the roof, eliminating the winter garden, with work on it postponed until after the cinema was up and running. Originally to be called the Picture House, like most PCT cinemas, it was given its locally appropriate name of The Regent a few months before opening. The most prominent feature of the front elevation on Queen's Road was the deep recess inside a slightly projecting arch, with the Renaissance Restaurant above the entrance hall. The arch (in black marble) was decorated with corner plaques, and a central panel in blue, white and green. The surrounding façade had two more panels set in the stonework, almost identical to the central one, with Venetian lanterns lower down. The frontage was doubly outlined in red bands.

Part of the Regent's inner main foyer and stairs to the stalls in 1921. The main entrance hall had walls of Caen stone. Beneath this lay the Ship Café, based on the wardroom of an eighteenth-century three-decker. Patrons had to descend to the stalls floor, which was entered from the back left because of the angle of the auditorium to the main entrance. However, a further entrance hall around the corner on North Street (at the corner of Windsor Street), which opened in a temporary state, was intended to be the main one for the stalls.

The cinema was first shown off to the press and other guests with a luncheon in the Renaissance Restaurant. The following day, Wednesday 27 July 1921, it opened to the public without ceremony at 11am with the film *A Yankee at the Court of King Arthur*, Basil Cameron's Orchestra, a live appearance by Norman Williams ('Britain's Most Popular Baritone') and a recital on the "straight" orchestral organ, made by William Hill & Son and Norman Beard, with three manuals and thirty-six speaking stops.

Among the first films shown were *The Mark of Zorro*, with Douglas Fairbanks, and *Pollyanna*, with Mary Pickford. The Regent advertised its own weekly newsreel, which showed the 1921 visit of the Prince of Wales to Brighton. Film shows initially started at 11am, Monday to Saturday. Separate Sunday morning concerts by Basil Cameron and his orchestra were part of the policy. However, by October, shows started at 1pm, the Sunday morning concerts were dropped and the price of the cheapest seats was raised from ninepence to one shilling (5p today). It had not got off to an entirely brilliant start.

The Regent in 1921 with its promenade at the back of the stalls and the view forward taking in one of the series of decorative panels set into the balcony soffit. The Regent was immediately applauded in the national and architectural press as by far the most remarkable cinema built in Britain to date, both internally and externally. The final cost was put at £400,000.

Described as an Adamesque adaptation of Roman classical motifs, the auditorium seated 2,200 people. Its fan shape was unusual at a time when most cinemas were rectangular, with parallel side walls. It was dominated by an immense curved proscenium arch, vividly decorated with a procession of figures in red and orange on a purple background. This was carried out by Lawrence Preston, Head of the Brighton School of Art.

Other decorative panels greeted stalls patrons as they entered the auditorium. A series designed by Walter Bayes, the Principal of the Westminster School of Art, was in the recesses in the underside of the balcony, seen from the back promenade. Their design was said 'to symbolise the spirit of buoyant, irresponsible youth.' Another vivid series, by Walpole Champneys, presented incidents from the story of Columbine and Harlequin in the foyer leading to the boxes in the balcony front.

Twelve years later, the distinguished Brighton-based architect and historian H.S. Goodhart-Rendel recalled in *The Architect and Building News* (3 February 1933): 'Here was a building the novelty and masterliness of which might have inaugurated a new age in Brighton's architectural repute... As it was first built it attracted the attention of Europe, it was visited by foreign architects of distinction, pictures of it were frequent in the art publications of all countries.'

The Regent in 1921: the view forward from the rear of the stalls and the view to the back.

The Regent in 1921 in all its short-lived glory. Note the huge area for the orchestra, and the curtains set far back on the stage. (Photograph: Chris Horlock.)

The Regent in 1921 with its original light fittings. The armchairs in the sectioned-off areas across the front of the balcony provided the best seats in the house. More armchairs can be seen in the side boxes.

The balcony's span of 110 feet was the largest of any theatre in the country. Its deeply curving front edge was richly decorated with repetitive panels, interspersed with the names of Shakespearean plays: *The Tempest, As You Like It, Julius Caesar,* etc.

The Regent was completed in 1923. The North Street entrance was built on a reduced scale, with the Georgian Room above it. The ballroom on the roof opened on 10 December, reached by lifts, with a lavish decor and space for up to 1,500 dancers. It became as much a feature of Brighton's leisure scene as the cinema below.

In July 1922, PCT hired the young American impresario Walter Wanger to manage the Regent, but he soon quarrelled with the board and received a huge settlement to leave. He became a notable film producer, and his 1963 epic *Cleopatra* had a lengthy run at the Regent. A leading film director, the late Roy Boulting, often recalled that he and his twin brother John first knew they had to become film makers after they were taken by their nanny to see the silent epic *The Four Horsemen of the Apocalypse* at the Regent in January 1923, and observed how it moved her to tears. Among the films the Boultings made was *Brighton Rock.*

The Regent continued to include top stage acts as well as films. In May 1927, for instance, the celebrated illusionist Maskelyne appeared twice daily for a week.

Above: The Regent in 1921
with a clear view of the
decorative frieze around the
proscenium arch. The main
curtains are decorated with
faces of comedy and tragedy.

Right: The Regent in late 1923
with the addition of the
Ballroom on the roof (courtesy
of Chris Horlock). The
Venetian lanterns to each side
of the canopy have made way
for advertising. At the far end is
the modest street entrance to
the Ship Café in the basement.
It could also be reached from
inside the cinema.

Left: The Academy scored a coup with the first showing in Brighton, from 1 May 1927 for two weeks, of the German epic *Metropolis*, the grandaddy of science-fiction films. The cinema greatly enlarged its orchestra, under Herbert Haywood, to play the full score as had been heard during its London run. Thirteen trains ran specially to Brighton each day from Worthing, Lewes and Haywards Heath. The residents in each of these areas had leaflets circulated to them promoting the film and the train service (*Metropolis* subsequently played for the week commencing Monday 5 September 1927 at the Cinema de Luxe).

Opposite top and above: the Regent after the fire. On the evening of 25 January 1929, the main feature, *Two Lovers*, had almost finished when a dressing room to the right of the stage was found to be ablaze. As a climax of fighting in a storm occupied the screen, the red glow at the top right of the proscenium arch was mistaken by many patrons for a special effect, until a tongue of flame swept across the picture. The cinema was evacuated and the safety curtain confined the flames to the stage, which was gutted, although smoke penetrated the auditorium and ruined the delicate decorations on the proscenium arch. It remained closed until 1 July 1929. The ballroom and restaurants were unaffected and remained open for business.

The new Gaumont combine had just acquired the Regent, and was fortunate in having three other halls in Brighton. The Academy and Court combined to show the Regent's programmes, while the live Hippodrome screened films on Sundays from 3 February to 23 June 1929. PCT's chief architect at the time, W.E. Trent, provided a new proscenium arch of conventional rectangular shape, with concealed lighting at the outer top and sides playing on a wide band with a zigzag pattern. The side boxes were removed and decorative grillework substituted. The balcony front was repainted, but the chandeliers and other hanging lights were removed in favour of smaller fittings and concealed illumination. A two-rank nine-manual Wurlitzer organ was installed. New seating and carpets appeared with conventional seats replacing armchairs at the front of the balcony. It was tasteful, more modern, but quite lacking the spirit and individuality of the original scheme. H. S. Goodhart-Rendel declared in 1933 that the Regent had been 'violated and vulgarised.'

After the Regent reopened, the Court closed on 5 November 1929 and was put up for sale. It had been the scene of the only other major Brighton cinema fire, in the early hours of Thursday 11 February 1926. The probable cause was a lighted cigarette end in one of the boxes on the left hand side of the auditorium. The £8,000 worth of damage was covered by insurance and the auditorium largely rebuilt, using the plans of architect F.C. Mitchell. It reopened on Monday 4 October 1926 with *The Flood*.

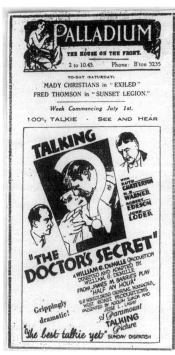

Over the years various unsuccessful attempts had been made to introduce talking pictures, mainly defeated by the difficulty of amplifying the sound. The Academy had installed Edison's Kinetophone by early 1914, an attempt which drew much initial interest. Historian Ian Grundy reports: 'An innovation at the Academy, which did not catch on, was kine-opera which was presented in 1920. This attempted to combine silent opera scenes with a pit orchestra and live singers behind the screen attempting to match their voices with the action of the film!'

By 1929, sound of an acceptable standard was available. Talking features made their bow at the Regent and the Palladium on the same day, Monday 1 July 1929, as shown in the advertisements above. The Regent followed its Al Jolson smash hit with such major sound pictures as *Bulldog Drummond* (with Ronald Colman) and Alfred Hitchcock's *Blackmail*. It still screened some silents as supporting features. The Palladium's first '100% Talkie' was followed by *Lucky Boy*, and other films generally inferior to those at the Regent. Both cinemas had Western Electric sound-on-film (rather than the more troublesome Vitaphone with sound on a separate disc). The Regent also added the sound newsreel, Movietone News, 'exclusive to this theatre'. For a time, it retained the orchestra to play live onstage between the films at evening shows only. The Wurlitzer organ was also regularly played.

The Academy was the third hall to introduce feature-length sound features when it opened the Gaumont production *High Treason* on 14 October. It soon added Gaumont Sound News, also 'exclusive to this theatre'. The tiny Tivoli on Western Road advertised 'Two short British talkies' from as early as 12 August. It installed a sound-on-disc system, and played the second run of *The Singing Fool* from 18 November (in 1932, an improved sound system was installed).

Within a year or so, sound had been added at the Cinema de Luxe and Prince's (both Western Electric) as well as the Court (British Acoustic), the Duke of York's (British Thomson-Houston) and all three Hove cinemas. New sound equipment was introduced at the Duke of York's on 26 May 1930 at a cost of £1,167.

Above: This view of the Scala, formerly the Queen's, dates from the second half of 1930, while that of the Princes is undated. The Scala in Western Road (courtesy of Chris Horlock) promotes its conversion to talkies while retaining an orchestra for showing the backlog of silent films, mostly as supporting features. The entrance is still divided into two sections with the current films advertised on the two fascias of the original shops, but it has been considerably modified while the Western Club (a billiard hall) is advertised above. As Dennis Williams has recalled, 'It was the practice of billiard players to tap the floor with their cues whenever a player made an exceptionally good shot, and these taps could be heard in the cinema, much to the annoyance of the management.' Williams adds that the screen was particularly small, without any tabs or decorative lighting, and was set high up, suggesting to him that the stalls floor may have been flat. After Saturday 20 February 1932, the Scala changed its name to Regal, and Dennis Williams remembers that a 'rising sun' neon display was installed above the entrance, and a V-shaped metal-framed sign was fitted midway over the top of the frontage extending out into the road, with the name Regal on both faces.

Below: The Princes in North Street advertises talkies, plus the ever-reliable draw of 'the little tramp' (photograph courtesy of Bob Elliston).

The main entrance of the Savoy, Brighton, at 75-79 East Street and the corner of Pool Valley, as it looked on opening in 1930 (photograph from Keith Skone's collection). The exterior was faced in glazed terracotta. The vertical name sign just to the right of the curving corner could be seen from some distance up King's Road. The cinema started out as a £250,000 scheme by Savoy Cinemas, designed by its regular architect F.C. Mitchell, replacing the enormous circular structure of Brill's Baths, which was demolished in early 1929.

When Savoy Cinemas became part of a newly formed major circuit, Associated British Cinemas (ABC), the Brighton scheme was redesigned by ABC's architect, W.R. Glen. Opened on Friday 1 August 1930, the Savoy was the first ABC hall to be built in England, the largest cinema ever built in Brighton (judged by seating capacity) and the second largest ever built by the circuit. The total number of seats was 2,567: 1,508 in the stalls and 1,059 in the balcony (although an even higher total of 2,630 was achieved after the Second World War). Built to match the Regent in splendour and scale, the Savoy had two restaurants, two cafés, two entrances, and a large and very unusual basement garage for 300 cars. One of the restaurants also functioned as a ballroom, but it was nowhere near as popular as that of the Regent.

Western Electric sound was installed and the Savoy opened with a seven-day run of an all-British, all-talking programme: two minor pictures from ABC's associated production arm (British International Pictures), *Loose Ends* and the musical featurette *Not So Quiet on the Western Front*, plus Quentin Maclean on the Savoy Wonder Organ, the Pathe Super News Gazette and Pathe Tone Weekly. There soon followed two-week runs of major attractions *All Quiet on the Western Front* and *The King of Jazz*, and later smash hits, such as *Grand Hotel*, in February 1933, also played a second week. Programmes changed on Fridays, with a 'midnight performance' every Wednesday at 11.45pm until the Second World War, aimed mainly at the shift workers at the Brighton locomotive works. No other Brighton cinema had regular late shows or started its new programme on a Friday.

Right: The Savoy had a prominent seafront entrance on Grand Junction Road or The Parade (photograph dated 26 January 1931, courtesy of Brighton History Centre, Brighton Museum). Each entrance had its restaurant and café above. This one was particularly noticeable to visitors, being floodlit at night and visible from the Palace Pier. Note the pylons with lamps on each side of the entrance steps. The side wall of the auditorium can be seen on the left, down Brill's Lane (the name recalling the former baths on the site). The manager's flat was also located above this entrance.

Below: the auditorium with its Compton organ console in the raised position – see overleaf.

Previous page, bottom: The auditorium of the Savoy, Brighton, in 1930, with its oriental decorative scheme inspired by the Royal Pavilion. It was designed by Charles Muggeridge, and executed by H.H. Martyn & Co. of Cheltenham. The ceiling was painted a light blue to suggest sky, while the central light fitting was a golden colour to indicate the sun flooding the auditorium with light. The panels on the upper wall showed landscapes, predominantly in shades of blue and pale yellow, which were Japanese in character and varied on each side. The intervening pilasters and cornice were painted to look like stone. The plaques below balcony level had Chinese motifs. Note the cutaway front to accommodate the projection beam from a box in the lower balcony (rather than at the back of the circle). Another sunburst was featured above the opening. The full-height panels alongside the proscenium were mirror images. There was a flight of exotic butterflies on the bottle-green stage curtains (butterflies became a standard feature in later ABC cinemas' curtains). Not visible is some vertical Chinese lettering in the top left hand corner of the curtain which translated as 'Our noble patrons are humbly beseeched not to despise this unworthy entertainment', reflecting the custom of a Chinese host to refer in deprecatory terms to what he has to offer his guests. Butterflies in a medley of tropical colours were also featured in the rose carpets which had a cobblestone pattern. The seats were upholstered in four different shades of velvet so that each had a different colour next to it. (Both pictures courtesy of Keith Skone.)

Opposite below: The Grand Theatre, North Road, Brighton, became the Grand Cinema Theatre on Monday 26 January 1931 following the run of a pantomime, *Cinderella*. Formerly the Hippodrome Circus of 1891, it was redesigned by architect Frank Matcham in 1894 and renamed the Eden Theatre. It became the Grand in 1904. This undated photograph (from Brighton History Centre at Brighton Museum) shows the magnificence of the exterior. Note the three statues above the entrance, along with the figures on the skyline and the rearing horsemen over the side entrances.

The Grand Theatre had shown some films while a variety theatre. The early 1930s was a very difficult time for live theatres (even the Theatre Royal was forced to close for a while in 1934) and overheads were considerably reduced by going over to films. The Grand had held 1,700 people, but it seated only 1,140 as a cinema because the gallery or upper circle was closed off (except on the day of greatest demand, Sunday). Installing the superior Western Electric sound system, the Grand started with two talkies, *Good News* and *The Ship from Shanghai*. It charged low admission prices (4d. to 1s.6d.) and showed mostly recent films on a late run, changing programmes mid-week. Dennis Williams observes: 'The projection room was built at the back of the gallery. The screen was very small indeed and always looked like a postage stamp in the middle of the large stage opening. Dark red tabs were hand drawn from the side of the stage. The footlights and house lights had no dimmers - they were just operated from a switch in the box.'

Another former theatre, the Court, found the going tough after it was relinquished by the Gaumont circuit. In January 1930 it was leased by Kingston Super Cinema Ltd, a company named after the cinema it ran in Kingston-on-Thames. W.W. Thompson then took it over for a premium of £500, and ran it from 19 April to 30 June 1931, when he was evicted for rent arrears of £960, having run this and another cinema in South London at a loss. Thompson was declared bankrupt on 8 October 1931. With 1,200 seats, the Court struggled on in other hands as a second-rate cinema.

The main Queen's Road foyer of the Regent was regularly decked out in themes that fitted its current main feature. Imitation petrol pumps flank the two box office windows on each side of the steps to help promote a minor film in 1931.

North Street in Portslade-by-Sea, showing on the left the 650-seat Pavilion cinema, which was the former Picturedrome as rebuilt and reopened in June 1932. (Courtesy of Trevor Povey.)

Previous page and opposite above: The Lido at Denmark Villas, Hove, by the railway station, was opened on 6 May 1932 by County Cinemas, a rapidly expanding chain. The building had started life on 23 December 1929 as a £70,000 ice rink, 180ft by 85ft, reputedly on part of the former Kinemacolor studio. Ice hockey was regularly featured but the rink failed. Conversion into a cinema, to the plans of Robert Cromie, took six weeks. The vast size of the interior resulted in a sea of 2,137 seats on a single sloping floor - almost as many as the Regent on two levels. The projection throw of 180 feet was one of the longest in the country and the rear seats were so far from the screen they had the lowest price. Passing trains could be heard as the building had not been designed to exclude their noise. The Wurlitzer organ was played on the opening night by Reginald Foort, while British actor Donald Calthrop, the villain of Hitchcock's *Blackmail*, was a celebrity guest. The first resident organist was Jack Hellier. A café, dance hall and car park were also included (Previous page, courtesy of Brighton History Centre at Brighton Museum; right, Tony Moss collection).

The opening of the Lido forced the closure of the Empire, Haddington Street. After the death of its original promoter, Harry Scriven, in 1926, his widow, Elizabeth, ran it with her son Eddie as the manager. In 1930, the cheap Electrocord sound-on-disc system was installed, soon becoming outmoded, and the cinema was acquired by a local figure, William Fuller, who renamed it the New Empire. It was licensed to seat 246: 188 on the ground floor and fifty-eight in the balcony. A fire occurred on Tuesday 13 January 1931 when, at around 9.25pm, a 2,000ft reel of silent film jammed in the gate of the projector. The chief operator, Thomas J. McNamara, seized the burning film with his hands and was almost blown out of the 10ft by 8ft operating box. The assistant operator, Albert Akehurst, released the metal shutters to cover the observation and projection holes, preventing fire from reaching the auditorium. The audience of about 100 left quietly within a minute. The only injuries were the burns to the two operators. The Empire carried on until 1932. Later, a Sainsbury's supermarket (currently the B-Wise clothing store) replaced it, with an entrance on Blatchington Road.

Opposite below: The Granada, Hove, shortly after its opening on 17 July 1933 on Portland Road, between Hove and Portslade, with the centre of Hove in the distance. There had been considerable interest in building a cinema on this site at the corner of School Road. Architect Cecil Masey submitted plans in 1928, followed by Webb & Ash in early 1932. The cinema was designed by H.L. Hemsley for a local company which went into partnership with the more experienced Mistlin & Lee, whose picture houses included the Granada, Dover. They gave the Granada name to the Hove cinema, despite its shortage of Spanish features. At the insistence of Nat Lee, the plans were modified by a specialist cinema architect, F.E. Bromige.

Built in brick with stone dressings, the Granada had an open tower on the corner over sixty feet high, which carried the cinema name. The auditorium was large, with 1,638 seats, and was equipped for cinema and theatre use with a flytower, a 22ft-deep stage behind a 45ft-wide proscenium, and five dressing rooms. The flytower was unfortunately exposed to full view by the car park next to it.

The interior decoration was executed by Winsor & Newton, but whether they also designed it remains unclear. The most striking decorative feature of the auditorium was the ten life-size figures along the side walls with outstretched arms that held light fittings. The walls were decorated with coloured butterflies and dragonflies (the stage curtains also featured butterflies). The ceiling was ten feet higher than it might have been, creating a lofty feeling. There was a café in the upper foyer. (Picture courtesy of Chris Horlock.)

Hove's only large purpose-built cinema, the Granada, opened with a weak double bill of *The Hawleys of High Street* and *The Kiss Before the Mirror*, supported by Don Rico and his Gipsy Girls Band, and the first resident organist, James Swift, on the two manual, five rank British-made Compton with an illuminated console that changed colour from within its wings of frosted glass. Anna Neagle was the special guest at the opening, along with the Mayor of Hove, who reputedly declared: 'I understand that the air conditioning is so perfect that even you people sitting in the sixpennies need not fear catching fleas from one another.'

Regrettably, no interior view of the auditorium has been located except for this close-up of Neville Meale at the Compton (courtesy of Tony Moss). Meale, who used his real name of Neville Taylor as the resident organist at the Granada, Hove, in 1934-5, went on to perform for the separate Granada Theatres chain as 'The Cheeky Chappie'.

On 18 June 1935 the Granadas at Dover and Hove were sold to the ABC circuit (which already operated the Savoy in Brighton). After being played for a period by the celebrated Robin Richmond, the Hove organ was taken out in 1936, modified, and installed at ABC's new Regal in Hammersmith. It ended up at the Napton Museum of Mechanical Music.

After the Lido, the Granada was the last straw for the small Empire in George Street. Owner S.W. Lewonski had belatedly installed Western Electric sound during the week of 11 December 1931. A 'horn chamber' (the space for the speaker behind the screen) had been built onto the stage end, reducing the exit space at the back of the building. The licensing authority required the two front rows of seats be removed from the centre block, and one row on each side to provide easier access to the front side exits. The Empire closed in early 1934 with Jack Hulbert in *Jack's the Boy*. It has been replaced by a new building, with two shops occupied in 2003 by the Select clothing store and Carters, domestic appliance suppliers.

Unrealised schemes for cinemas in Hove in the 1930s included a £150,000 cinema/theatre with restaurant by architects Verity & Beverley for Dr E. Distin Maddick, approved in March 1936; and a year later, a project for northern Hove, at the junction of Hangleton Road and Applesham Avenue, by F.E. Bromige, who had worked on the Granada.

The Astoria Brighton opened on Thursday 21 December 1933, occupying 10-17 Gloucester Place, including the parade of shops and flats extending to the corner with Blenheim Place. The prominent site, on a main route to the seafront and Palace Pier, was first envisaged for a Plaza cinema in 1932 by a syndicate headed by J. Henson Infield, who controlled the *Sussex Daily News* and was involved with Brighton's Theatre Royal. F.W. Griggs, a builder, was a partner who would undertake the construction. Infield subsequently teamed up with veteran exhibitor E.E. 'Teddy' Lyons, who had opened the Academy, West Street, in 1910 with Infield as chairman and sold it in 1926.

The Astoria was designed by Edward A. Stone. The first delivery of steel took place on 17 July 1933 so that it was completed in five months. The rather dull façade was faced in white stone blocks. The entrance block projected slightly, with a rectangular-shaped canopy extending over the pavement. The pay box was open to the street in American style. The frames and fluted panels in the three round-arched windows were in a bronze green colour. The cinema name was mounted in a slight recess, and emphasised by neon. Extending to the left were ground floor shops, a first floor tea room and second floor accommodation including a manager's flat. These masked the bulk of the auditorium. The flytower with the stage door and scenery dock was along Blenheim Place. The 20ft-deep stage had four dressing rooms.

The entrance hall (right) relied on combing of the plaster surface of the ceiling and walls for much of its effect. The walls were brown with a pinkish tinge. The column seen right was in dull silver, capped by bands in dark green and white, while the ceiling had a dull gold colour. The one staircase to the balcony at the rear had its solid balustrade ending in a curve, reinforcing the curves in the pattern on the floor.

The Astoria opened with the huge hit *The Private Life of Henry VIII,* supported by the short *Santa's Workshop,* a stage show, and T. Guy Hindell at the Compton organ. (Pictures courtesy of Bruce Peter.)

This page and opposite: The interior of the Astoria was refreshingly modern, and a startling contrast to the Savoy and Regent (photographs from the Keith Skone collection, right, and Bruce Peter, left). Architect Edward A. Stone relied on leading decorators to handle his interiors: nobody was specifically credited here, but Richard Gray declared (in *Picture House*, No. 26, Summer 2001) that 'the work of interior designers Henri and Laverdet was clearly evident and similar to their surviving interior at the Whitehall theatre in London'. (This team had also collaborated with Stone on the Astoria cinemas at Streatham and Finsbury Park in London.)

The views of the Astoria's auditorium show the unusual French art deco style adopted. The colour scheme was predominantly golden, with the decorative attention focused on the proscenium arch and splay walls. The bas relief frieze above the arch depicted nude figures in a stylised setting. The decorative plaster grilles over the side exits concealed the organ chamber on the right side. The ornamental forms were painted in wine-red, white, blue and gold. The seats were rose-coloured. The side walls further back were elaborately textured in fan shapes. The Compton organ had a cascade-style illuminated console that changed colours and, very unusually, came up on a lift in the centre of the stage (it was later moved to the more conventional position in the centre of the orchestra pit). The pit was covered by an extended stage with a vividly decorated surface visible only from the balcony.

This was the first in a new circuit of Astoria cinemas masterminded by E.E. Lyons. He opened Astorias at Purley, Surrey, in April 1934 and, five days before his death on 9 August 1934, at Cliftonville, Kent. He was also linked to the aborted Astoria, Worthing. The Brighton and Cliftonville cinemas were acquired in February 1935 by the ABC circuit. This Astoria was able to book strong new films as the third most important cinema in Brighton, after ABC's Savoy and the Regent, until the Odeon opened in West Street in 1937. It then became part of ABC's 'B' circuit, booking less attractive films that could not obtain playing time on the main circuit.

Opposite and above: Opened on Thursday 1 February 1934 as an inexpensive (£7,838) adaptation of stables by architect Andrew Mather, the Odeon at Kemp Town, a district east of the town centre, was a thoroughly undistinguished early addition to what rapidly became a national circuit of major significance (In 1933, Odeon had briefly contemplated a site at Moulsecoomb in the northwest of Brighton).

Situated at 38 St George's Road, at the corner with Paston Place, the Odeon seated 958 in a stadium arrangement, which allowed a lower ceiling but reduced the capacity. There were 556 seats in the lower front section, and 402 in the raised and separate rear section called the balcony. The suspended light fittings were at the sides to avoid the beam from the projectors. The theatre (Odeon always called its cinemas 'theatres') opened with a British comedy *A Cuckoo in the Nest*, starring Tom Walls and Ralph Lynn. On Friday, a few variety acts were included in the programme. No café was provided. It played mostly split-week runs of new films a few weeks after their appearance in the centre of Brighton.

The views opposite were taken in mid-1935 by Odeon's contract photographer, John Maltby. By then a vertical sign reading 'Cinema' with neon overlay had been added on the corner, to be visible from the seafront down the street opposite. The vertical Odeon sign, also with neon attached, looks towards the centre of Brighton. The original horizontal Odeon sign has no neon, and is floodlit from the canopy.

Kemp Town already had the tiny King's Cliff Cinema in Sudeley Place, a former congregational chapel, opened in 1920 with 300 seats (raised the following year to 378 by demolishing an old tea room at the back of the hall). This survived the arrival of the Odeon. Remembered by Dennis Williams as having 'the most unintelligible sound and breakdowns [that] appeared with unfailing regularity', it passed to new owners in 1939 who made some improvements.

The picture above shows members of the Kemp Town Odeon's Mickey Mouse Club lining up after a show in the summer of 1937. Like most large cinemas, the Odeon ran children's clubs on Saturday mornings to inculcate the habit of cinema-going at an early age. Clubs also carried out good deeds and promoted good behaviour.

The Rothbury, Franklin Road, Portslade-by-Sea, shortly before opening on Tuesday 27 March 1934. With 550 seats, this single-floor adaptation of a partly-built assembly hall looked very much a cinema, with some art deco fittings. It had a café lounge off the foyer. It competed for local custom with the much smaller, independently-run Pavilion. The name 'Rothbury' was chosen by the builder, A.L. Middleton, after his place of birth in Northumberland. He was one of the directors, together with Oscar Deutsch and F. Stanley Bates, who were busy setting up the first Odeon cinemas. The architect was George Coles, who subsequently became a main Odeon architect. (Photographs from the Keith Skone collection.)

The Rothbury. Oscar Deutsch was chairman of the owning company, attended the opening and claimed it as part of his then small Odeon circuit. The lettering in the Rothbury name and in the vertical sign reading 'Cinema' is in the Odeon style. However, the absence of the Odeon name suggests that Middleton had the upper hand. Deutsch and Bates soon severed their connection, leaving Middleton to run the cinema by himself. He recruited Mrs I. Merriman Langdon, lessee of the Ritz cinema at Seaford, and in 1938 she signed a twenty-one-year lease to take it over. Although it played films long after their first run in Brighton and Hove, its modernity and good location gained it a steady local trade.

On 15 April 1935, the Palladium on Brighton's seafront was taken over by Oscar Deutsch's fast-expanding Odeon circuit. Andrew Mather, the architect of the Odeon, Kemp Town, and others for the circuit, slapped on a modern art deco frontage involving the addition of much neon, and a curvaceous canopy that stretched over the pavement, fitted with bright lights on the underside. The result was eye-catching and made up for the narrow width. The foyer was also completely modernised but the auditorium remained very much the same. Although reseated, it was something of an anti-climax to those expecting a modern treatment throughout. The cinema closed for two weeks for the interior changes to take place, and reopened with the Odeon name and a midnight performance on 8 June 1935. For its first attraction, it had the British premiere of Columbia's Edward G. Robinson gangster comedy *Passport to Fame* (*The Whole Town's Talking*).

Left: Here the Odeon name has been plucked off the top of the façade, and the Palladium name reinstated on top of the canopy. The change took place on 28 November 1937, three weeks before a brand new Odeon opened in West Street. (Both photographs by John Maltby.)

Opposite above: This is the Palladium's auditorium after it became an Odeon (John Maltby).

Opposite below: One cinema that had little scope to change its external appearance was the Cinema de Luxe, the former Theatre de Luxe, seen here *c.* 1935 (courtesy of Brighton History Centre, Brighton Museum).

The dazzling reconstruction of the former Scala/Regal in Western Road, photographed by Mr Cox, one of its projectionists, at Easter 1937 (courtesy of Brighton History Centre, Brighton Museum). It was essentially a new cinema when it reopened with the sophisticated name of the Curzon on 3 August 1936, after eleven weeks of work to plans by architect James Morrison for its proprietor, Kenneth A. Nyman. The perforated canopy above the big Curzon sign was a modern touch, later seen more conspicuously at the Regal, Walton-on-Thames, and Odeon, East Ham. Bands of parallel vertical neon strips blaze away on each side, curving over the top of the building.

The name Plaza had been intended until the last minute, according to Dennis Williams, who recalls that the garden of the first house in Montpelier Road (off to the left) was bought to extend the cinema. As this land was higher, to reduce excavation costs the cinema gained a 'dished' stalls floor that curved up towards the screen (a familiar device on the Continent but very rare in Britain). Four circular plaques in the foyer had Walt Disney characters painted on them soon after the reopening. The one failing was the retention of the old projectors and sound equipment, resulting in poor sound. An excellent location in a busy shopping area overcame the low capacity (656 seats in 1949), along with its booker's shrewd eye for booking and re-booking recent box-office hits at the right time for a full week. It advertised itself as 'Brighton and Hove's Intimate Kinema' and opened with the recent Fred Astaire/Ginger Rogers musical *Top Hat*, indicative of the kind of family entertainment in which it specialised (no gangster or cowboy pictures). The Curzon shared the Paramount newsreel first run with the Grand, requiring it to be transported back and forth between the two cinemas.

The owners of the Tivoli, almost opposite the Curzon, reacted by making major improvements: a new canopy, a central revolving door, a completely redecorated auditorium with new seats (350, with padded arm rests), carpets, festoon curtain and projectors.

54

The Gaiety, Lewes Road (from Chris Horlock's collection). It opened on Saturday 24 April 1937 with the Fred Astaire/Ginger Rogers musical *Swing Time*, plus the world premiere of a Coronation film, *The King's People* (Dennis Williams recalls that the projectionists missed out one reel of the main feature and the chief projectionist, who made matters worse by tacking it on the end, was sacked). Situated at the corner with Hollingdean Road, the Gaiety was designed by Frederick W. Morgan. Unquestionably, it had the most radical frontage of all the cinemas in the area with its six 53ft-high concrete fins, their curved tops complementing the curved frontage that was brilliantly lit by neon at night, above a full-width canopy. The foyer had a streamlined island pay box with a long corridor leading to the fan-shaped auditorium with 1,206 seats in stalls and balcony. There was an enormous circular dome at the top of the staircase to the balcony, lit up with constantly changing colours.

The cinema was initiated by Arthur Edwards, but subsequently involved Randolph E. Richards, who ran six cinemas in Eastbourne, Hastings, Bexhill-on-Sea and St Leonards-on-Sea - the best of which were called Gaiety. These enjoyed first runs of new films, but the Brighton Gaiety played second or third run after the city centre. Besides being strikingly modern, it had the advantage over some of its rivals of a car park at the rear for 300 vehicles.

The arrival of the Gaiety spurred its immediate rivals to make improvements. The Arcadia, also in Lewes Road, gained a semi-circular metal canopy. Mothers were known to use the long corridor to the auditorium as a crèche, popping out periodically to check up on their offspring. The Duke of York's closed for the week of 21 June 1937. The interior was redecorated, a new screen with new festooned curtains was installed, the sound system was improved, and 750 new seats replaced the former 890. Neon lighting was introduced on the side walls for what was claimed to be the first time in any cinema in the country. It was certainly a novelty but, as Dennis Williams clearly remembers, it did not dim and had to be switched on and off, creating a rather crude impression. The cinema declared that its long-running slogan, 'Bring her to the Duke's - it's fit for a Duchess', was never more apt.

Above: The Odeon on West Street, Brighton, at the northern corner with Little Russell Street, opened on Saturday 18 December 1937. It was part of the redevelopment of that side of West Street after the building line had been set back.

This cinema was originally designed by the Andrew Mather practice for an entrepreneur, H.H. Weingott, who would have called it the Forum (decades later, the wiring charts in the projection room still carried the Forum name). It was identified as an Odeon scheme by June 1936, and submitted for approval in January 1937. It occupied an excellent site in the centre of Brighton, on the 'tripper track' between the railway station and seafront. On the other corner of Little Russell Street stood the S.S. Brighton, a much bigger building than the Odeon, opened in June 1934 as a swimming pool and converted in October 1935 to an ice rink and conference/sports centre. The Odeon's basic cost was £48,000; the S.S. Brighton cost £80,000.

The frontage was designed in cream faienceware, with green bands and a base of black stippled glass - which fitted in broadly with the established Odeon style and continued the streamlined 1930s look of the S.S. Brighton with its tiled frontage, colour bands and canopy. The main Odeon sign might have been squeezed within the six vertical ribs (which recall those of the Odeon, Aylesbury, another Mather scheme taken over by the circuit) but two matching signs were placed on the wings as at the Odeon, Barnet, also an inherited scheme. The right-angled banding at each side added strength to the façade, especially when emphasised by green and yellow neon at night. The weak points were the placing of old-fashioned curlicued grillework between the ribs and the cone-like finials above them.

The Odeon circuit believed simply in showing films in modern and comfortable surroundings. Although there was a modest café, no restaurant, dance hall nor organ was included, and the backstage facilities were limited to one or two dressing rooms for the odd personal appearance.

Below: The auditorium of the Odeon, Brighton, with its vividly coloured inner curtains showing a winged horse and charioteer. The canopy connecting the splay walls had dramatic impact, pierced by the line of inner-lit circular openings, and the concealed lighting of the proscenium surround was effective, but this was a dull scheme compared to the best Odeons. The decoration was gold and brown and the dado was Australian walnut. An octagonal Odeon clock was placed on each side wall. (Both photos by John Maltby for Odeon.)

Oscar Deutsch had acquired the Palladium a short distance away, but this was not large enough to secure major first-run films. Taking over the Forum scheme solved the problem, and gave him a modern cinema that would be far more inviting to contemporary audiences. It was bigger than it looked, packing in 1,920 seats (1,236 in the stalls and 684 in the balcony). From the start, the Odeon had a stream of top attractions booked for national release through the circuit, putting it on a par with the Savoy and the Regent as one of Brighton's three leading cinemas. It was given special treatment from time to time. The highly topical drama *Q Planes*, starring Ralph Richardson and Laurence Olivier, had its Grand European Premiere run from Thursday 29 June 1939, ten days before its opening in London. The Odeon's films would subsequently play at the Palladium and Lido, Hove.

This was one of several Odeons with a Car Club. Formed in the summer of 1938, it held rallies and treasure hunts and had its own badge for affixing to car radiators.

At the end of the decade, at least one entrepreneur, H.E. King, thought there was scope for a further cinema on a corner of West Street, together with a restaurant, chain store, bars, 200 flats, basement garage and air raid shelter! The outbreak of war killed any chance of proceeding.

Like the Palladium-turned-Odeon, the Princes in North Street used the full height of its narrow frontage to gain attention. A high Continental-style canopy is seen being installed in early 1938 (photograph by John Maltby, from the Keith Skone collection) while the night-time view with its blaze of neon, dated 12 March 1938 (courtesy of Chris Horlock), shows bands of neon plunging towards the narrow entrance. The old-fashioned shops to each side provide a piquant contrast (This was not the first use of neon on the exterior: a report indicates that 300 feet of neon lighting in horizontal strips on a black background had been introduced for Whitsun in 1933).

REX

BRIGHTON'S

NEWS

THEATRE

NORTH ROAD, BRIGHTON

Lessee & Manager : JOHN C. HOWE
Phone : Brighton 4889

Continuous 2 till 11 p.m. (including Sundays)

NINETY MINUTES OF PERFECT SCREEN ENTERTAINMENT

Opening Night :
Saturday, 30th July
At 7 o'clock

Saturday, 30th July
FIVE DAYS

GAUMONT BRITISH NEWS
(v)

UNIVERSAL NEWS
(v)

THE OLD MILL
Walt Disney's Silly Symphony in Colour (u)

STRANGER THAN FICTION
No. 28   Interest (v)

WED TIME STORY
COMEDY   (v)

HIGH, WIDE AND DASHING
MUSICAL   (v)

LOUIS v. SCHMELING FIGHT
(v)

Thursday, 4th Aug.
FOR THREE DAYS

GAUMONT BRITISH NEWS
(U)

UNIVERSAL NEWS
(U)

IT NEVER RAINS
COMEDY   (v)

HOLLYWOOD SCREEN TEST
(U)

SECRETS OF LIFE
No. 13.   The Tawny Owl
(U)

STRANGER THAN FICTION
No. 27. Interest
(U)

PLENTY OF MONEY AND YOU
COLOURED CARTOON
(U)

PRICES - - 4d., 6d. and 1/-
CAR PARK ADJOINING 6d.

The Rex News Theatre at the bottom of North Road opened on Saturday 30 July 1938. The former Coronation/Troxy closed on Sunday 3 July 1938 to gain a modern frontage featuring a bold neon display that emphasised the word NEWS rather than the name Rex. Although on a tram route, it was too out of the way to draw the passing trade to its ninety minutes of low-priced 'perfect entertainment... continuous from 2 until 11.' It seems to have lasted only until Saturday 26 November 1938. (Photograph courtesy of Chris Horlock.)

The news policy had been tried before. From 7 September to 4 October 1931, the Academy in West Street became the Tatler News Theatre. With 1,017 seats, it was too large for such a policy, and reverted to feature films, regaining its Academy name on 18 January 1932. Other news theatres had been planned: at the Clarence Room suite of the Metropole Hotel (1933); for General Cinema Theatres at 14-18 High Street to plans by Cecil Masey (1935); at the rear of the Arlington Hotel, Charles Street, to plans by Heinrich Emil Mendelssohn (1936) (possibly the same as a 1937 scheme at Charles Street/Manchester Street, designed by news theatre specialist Alister G. MacDonald); and for 139-142 North Street (MacDonald again, 1938).

The Rex became a motorcycle shop, Redhill Motors, from 1949. The former auditorium has very recently been replaced by thirteen one-bedroom flats and, as illustrated on page 21, the entrance is being restored in 2003 to resemble its original 1911 appearance.

Opposite and above: The Academy, West Street. Although the secondary Gaumont hall, the Academy did good business thanks to its excellent location and first call on recent hits at the Regent. In 1938, Gaumont chief architect W.E. Trent brought it up to date with the Odeon and other new buildings on the reconstructed side of West Street. First came the complete modernisation of the auditorium under the supervision of locally-born architect A.E. Potter – this was carried out at night and in the mornings from late May without closing the cinema. The photograph above (from Chris Horlock's collection) is dated 8 June 1938. Unfortunately, no images of the original proscenium have come to light. Then came the transformation of the exterior (seen opposite). The pictures show the building before work started (courtesy of Brighton History Centre, Brighton Museum), and nearing completion in early March 1939 (courtesy of Chris Horlock). The GB emblem identifies the cinema as part of the Gaumont British chain. The new look is hardly an improvement.

W. E. Trent also drew up plans in the autumn of 1937 for a new Gaumont cinema on Old London Road at the outlying district of Patcham. It would seat 1,350 and serve the new housing estates there. There had been interest in the area in March 1936 when Hughes, Hain & Co. were the architects for a cinema between the Patcham bypass road and the old London Road. Then, in April 1939, F.E. Bromige was appointed architect for a cinema on Old London Road to seat 1,500. The Second World War put an end to Patcham's hopes of having its own local picture house.

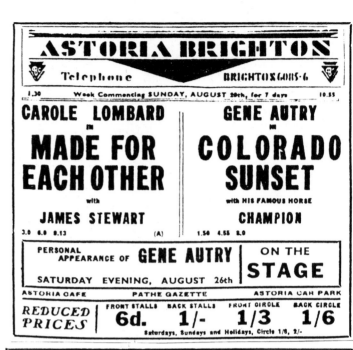

ASTORIA BRIGHTON

Telephone   BRIGHTON GARS·6

1.30   Week Commencing SUNDAY, AUGUST 20th, for 7 days   10.55

CAROLE LOMBARD in   **GENE AUTRY** in

MADE FOR EACH OTHER   **COLORADO SUNSET**

with   with HIS FAMOUS HORSE

JAMES STEWART   **CHAMPION**

3.0 6.0 9.13   (A)   1.50 4.55 8.0

PERSONAL APPEARANCE of **GENE AUTRY**   ON THE

SATURDAY EVENING, AUGUST 26th   **STAGE**

ASTORIA CAFE   PATHE GAZETTE   ASTORIA CAR PARK

REDUCED PRICES   FRONT STALLS   BACK STALLS   FRONT CIRCLE   BACK CIRCLE

6d.   1/-   1/3   1/6

Saturdays, Sundays and Holidays, Circle 1/6, 2/-

ASTORIA, BRIGHTON

EXCLUSIVE

STRAIGHT FROM HOLLYWOOD

On the stage in Person

GENE AUTRY

The World Famous Singing Cowboy and Company at 8. 45 p.m.

TO - NIGHT

Gene Autry will arrive at Brighton Station at 7 p.m.

COME AND WELCOME YOUR SINGING COWBOY STAR

In August 1939, the Astoria offers the added attraction of a personal appearance by singing star Gene Autry, not at a children's show, but at the evening performance. Autry's arrival by train at 7pm was publicised so that fans could greet him at the station (Champion, his 'wonder horse', had already sailed for home). The following week, Tod Slaughter, the star of a minor new crime drama, *The Face at the Window,* was advertised as making a personal appearance at every show in a particularly elaborate attempt to boost attendances. Note the reduced prices, nearly half those of the Savoy and indicative of the Astoria's struggle for customers.

three

World War Two
and Post-War Peak

British cinemas were never more appreciated than during the Second World War as the safest haven from grim reality, and they were never more popular than in the postwar years of austerity and shortages. Attendances nationally reached an all-time peak of 1,635 million in 1946 as people celebrated victory and sought relaxation in one of the few forms of entertainment available.

After war was declared on Sunday 3 September 1939, cinemas, theatres and other places of entertainment were closed nationwide as a precaution against bombing raids. All Brighton cinema staff attended lectures on Air Raid Precautions (ARP) at the Astoria. No raids occurred, and Brighton's cinemas were allowed to reopen on Saturday 9 September. However, early closing at 10 p.m. was required. At most cinemas, the previously advertised programmes came on a week late. Some of the films had a marked topicality: the Savoy offered *Confessions of a Nazi Spy* while the Palladium and Lido presented *Idiot's Delight*, a drama about war erupting in Europe.

Brighton became a 'restricted area', with most hotels closed or taken over by the military. A curfew was imposed an hour after sunset from Tuesday 9 July 1940 on the area south of North Street and Western Road, much to the irritation of the Odeon's manager, who felt that it should have affected all the town's cinemas or none. This resulted in the Odeon having to start its last show of the day much earlier. (From December 1942 Brighton cinemas had to finish by 9.30 p.m. because the buses stopped running then to save fuel and wear on the tyres.)

The district's first air raid happened on 15 July 1940. Two months later, the heaviest casualties of any local raid occurred at Kemp Town, with many of the dead and injured being patrons at the Odeon there.

Cinemas were considered one of the best places to shelter, safe from anything but a direct hit (the Savoy advertised an 'Official Air Raid Shelter in Basement', no doubt referring to its underground garage). As elsewhere in the country, performances were initially halted for the manager to make an onstage announcement of any air raid warning; but there were so many false alerts that slides were soon shown over the film on the screen instead (John Fernee recalls that, at the Princes, stencilled lettering lit up on each side of the screen in two small boxes, the upper one to warn of an air raid and the lower one to announce 'Raiders passed'). Patrons could leave if they chose, but they did not receive a refund and the idea of going home in the blackout during a possible air raid was not an attractive one. Programmes were rescheduled so that the first feature came on earlier, enabling patrons to get home in daylight or stay to see the second feature. Power cuts sometimes interrupted the films, but audiences would join in a sing-song, led by the manager or organist. Cinemas would often stay open after closing time to shelter patrons if an air raid was still in progress. At the Duke of York's, firemen from the station next door were given reserved seats - if they became needed, the manager flashed the house lights and the men would rush to their posts.

Cinemas could not put on any external illumination and had to black out their glass doors (but Dennis Williams recalls that the Curzon repainted its foyer light blue so that the fluorescent glow from two ultra-violet lamps provided just enough illumination to avoid covering the glass doors).

The weaker halls were forced to shut down, at least temporarily. The Court closed on Saturday 29 June 1940 with the Laurel and Hardy comedy *Jailbirds* and the Grand followed on the last Saturday of September 1940 with *I Take This Woman*, and a western, *Rawhide* (even though some further programmes were advertised). The Grand made a comeback with variety shows from Monday 21 July 1941 and continued as a live theatre until February 1955. It became a showroom for Beven Funnell, the reproduction furniture company, until a fire in June 1961 gutted the auditorium. It was demolished, and today the NCP car park and the Tower Point building occupy most of the site. As if to compensate for the loss of the Grand as a cinema, the newly opened Imperial Theatre, after a hopeless struggle to put on live shows, turned to films in 1943, beginning nearly twenty years as a significant, second rank central Brighton picture house.

The Odeon chain closed the seafront Palladium on Saturday 26 October 1940 after a week's run of the Shirley Temple film *The Blue Bird*, stating it was impossible to draw reasonable audiences at that time. An independent operator reopened it on Sunday 2 August 1942, offering some first runs of very minor films but mainly showing recent films on second or third runs. The Arcadia in Lewes Road also closed in 1940, but reopened under new management in 1944. At Kemp Town, the King's Cliff closed temporarily in 1941, then indefinitely from May 1943.

Nevertheless, most of Brighton's cinemas were well-attended, whether they showed escapist fare like Technicolor Hollywood musicals or rousing films about the war and the home front (*Dangerous Moonlight*, an air combat drama with the memorable theme music of Richard Addinsell's Warsaw Concerto, was a particular favourite, often revived by the Curzon). Provincial premieres, often concurrent with London, took place, including *My Son, My Son* at the Savoy and *That Night in Rio* at the Odeon. Some pictures, such as *For Whom the Bell Tolls* at the Odeon West Street, were popular enough to be booked for two weeks, while *Gone with the Wind* stayed for three at the Astoria.

One small change possible during the Second World War was the renaming of the Lido, Hove, from Sunday 30 July 1944 as an Odeon, reflecting the fact that the County circuit had been amalgamated with the Odeon chain in September 1939.

In 1945 the Regent (left) shows how cluttered its frontage had become. In 1946 the Granada, Hove (right) shows its affiliation with the ABC circuit via the small triangle sign on the right. Someone is closely studying the display of stills which was one of the most potent ways of drawing people in.

ASTORIA

BRIGHTON · Phone : Brighton 6085

Commencing SUNDAY, JUNE 16th

David O. Selznick's Production
In Technicolor

GONE WITH THE WIND

Starring CLARK GABLE as Rhett Butler

LESLIE · CLIVIA
HOWARD · De HAVILLAND

and presenting

VIVIEN LEIGH as Scarlett O'Hara

A Metro-Goldwyn-Mayer Release

ALL SEATS BOOKABLE !

AFTERNOONS at 1.30. DOORS OPEN at 1 o'clock. 3/6 All Parts.
EVENINGS at 6.30. DOORS OPEN at 6 o'clock. 3/6 and 4/6.

Don't Miss The Film Event of the Age !

Amid the worries of that first year of the 'phoney war', just before the first air raids took place, Brighton was one of only twelve towns outside London to show the most eagerly awaited film in a decade. *Gone with the Wind* opened on Sunday 16 June 1940 with twice-daily showings at the Astoria at increased prices. Its first release was very limited because most cinemas refused to show it on the terms demanded by its distributor as they would set a dangerous precedent. The film ran for three weeks and some local cinemagoers may have held out in the hope of seeing it later at normal prices, since a unique low-price engagement in Blackpool lasted twelve weeks.

In general, the Astoria struggled for good films to show. In 1941 its bookings featured a French film that was a hit in London (*Amok*), reissues (including *The Ghost Goes West*) and minor new films (the provincial premiere of something called *Sis Hopkins*).

When *Gone with the Wind* returned to Brighton on a full ABC circuit release, it was booked into the Astoria again, still at increased prices. It played from 16 August 1942, announced for two weeks but held over for four, setting a Brighton record. However, its longest run at the Astoria was in the 70mm version shown from 29 September 1968 to 18 January 1969. It returned in 1975 from 23 October to 19 November.

The Cinema de Luxe is seen closed, some years after a fire which was unrelated to the War. The former Theatre de Luxe seated 529 in the 1930s. It was taken over from Electric Theatres (1908) by T. Easten Rutherford, *c.* 1934. Dennis Williams, who knew it from 1929 onwards, recalls a long, narrow hall with one central aisle and rows of seats extending to the side walls. The ceiling was higher in the front of the auditorium, dropping further back to enclose a spacious projection room with a very short throw to the screen. 'There was no stage and the screen, which had rounded corners to the end, was surrounded by a flat "picture frame" proscenium about two feet wide which appeared to be made of translucent cloth behind which were low wattage lamps coloured red and controlled by a dimmer. The tabs were plain dark red velvet and motor operated. The seats were poorly upholstered and covered in dark red plush, very uncomfortable. The walls were decorated in Jacobean ovals and on each side were a number of translucent shades containing red lamps which always appeared to be too bright. The entire colour scheme was dark red, and no redecoration took place during my memories. As the screen had not been replaced or resprayed within living memory, the screen illumination was pretty dismal but the picture was sharp and steady and the sound was excellent. The rake was fairly steep for a cinema without a circle. The auditorium clock was large and square with an illuminated advert for the *Brighton Evening Argus*. The Cinema de Luxe always ran seven-day programmes, which was unusual for small private halls which usually had three changes a week. The news was third-run Pathé Gazette.'

The cinema was empty on the morning of Wednesday 25 March 1942 - except for the resident black cat, Spud - when fire broke out at the screen end. The blaze took three hours to extinguish. The only casualty was Spud. The films in the projection room were undamaged and their titles - *Behind the News* and *Petticoat Politics* - faded away over the years on the display above the entrance while the remains of the auditorium became a car park. Capital and Provincial News Theatres put up an announcement in late 1958/early 1959 that it would open a news and cartoon cinema here, but the site ultimately became part of a large office block with shops at street level. The building next door still stands in 2003 as a branch of the HSBC bank. (Picture courtesy of Bob Elliston.)

Above: The Odeon Kemp Town (courtesy of Brighton History Centre, Brighton Museum). Brighton's worst air raid occurred early in the war, on Saturday 14 September 1940. Many of the deaths and injuries happened at the Odeon. A few minutes into an early afternoon screening of a minor film called *It Could Happen To You*, the show was interrupted by manager Cyril D. Huxtable who announced an air raid warning, but the audience of nearly 300 remained in place. Shortly afterwards, a lone German raider being chased by a Spitfire dropped a number of bombs, one of which landed in the right hand front corner of the auditorium near the rows of sixpenny seats and exploded, exposing the sky through the shattered roof and splitting the screen from top to bottom. Usherette Gladys Nash told Brighton historian John Montgomery: 'It was the most horrible experience of my life. A bomb came through the roof and exploded in front of the screen. There were children all around me, dead.' One nine-year-old who survived, Tony Bishop, recalled in 1997: 'There was a terrifying rattle, almost like a shower of giant hailstones landing on the roof of the cinema. In a split second, the rattle was followed by an enormous explosion and I saw the soldier in front of me had no head.' The number of young victims was increased because the Saturday morning Mickey Mouse Club had been suspended and the remaining chapters of the serial transferred to Saturday afternoon performances.

The number of victims varies according to sources. At the time, it was claimed that the raid had taken fifty-two lives, with severe injuries to eighty-five other people. The actual number of deaths from the bomb falling on the Odeon seems to have been eight children and six adults, many of whom died later in hospital.

Below: The Odeon Kemp Town, reinstated after the bombing (courtesy of Brighton History Centre, Brighton Museum). Following the attack, Odeon chief Oscar Deutsch promptly invited the staff to take a week's holiday in the country at Cookham, near the circuit's wartime headquarters, and arranged for them to visit the set of *Major Barbara* at Denham Studios where they were posed with its stars, Wendy Hiller and Rex Harrison, for a photograph that appeared in the Brighton press. Manager Huxtable was appointed to run the Odeon, Marlow, while the rest of the staff were temporarily assigned to the Odeon and Palladium in the centre of Brighton, and to the Lido at Hove. Up to 120 men went to work immediately on repairing and modernising the building at a stated cost of £8,000 to plans drawn up by Leonard Allen, successor to the original architect, the late Andrew Mather. The main steel girder, roof and ceiling had to be replaced; all glass light fittings were removed (new suspended fittings were made of a material that would flutter to the ground), 400 seats were reupholstered and a new sound system installed. Lily Deutsch, the wife of Oscar and advisor on Odeon decorative treatments, selected a rose-coloured scheme, while an Odeon subsidiary, Decorative Crafts, supplied the colourful inner tableau curtain showing a 'mountain pass' design and a front curtain in gold and silver festoons. The Odeon re-opened at 1.45 p.m. on Boxing Day with the hit Bob Hope/Bing Crosby comedy *Road to Singapore* for a three-day run, and Oscar Deutsch arranged an informal dinner for all the workmen involved to thank them for their efforts, a gesture that the Odeon press corps brought to the attention of the local press. The company also placed a special advertisement in the press to thank Bostel Brothers of West Street, Brighton, for their services.

The Savoy in the centre of Brighton had a near miss. As related in David Rowland's book *The Brighton Blitz*, on 29 November 1940 an incendiary bomb crashed through the roof to land in one corner of the auditorium, but a report stated: 'All but a few patrons, close to where the bomb fell, retained their seats and the film was not interrupted.'

Above: The Imperial Theatre in North Street, Brighton, on opening night as a live theatre (photograph from the Chris Horlock collection). It was built for a company headed by Jack Buchanan and Ralph Lynn, but work was interrupted by the Second World War. The architect was Sam Beverley and its interior design has been attributed to John Alexander. The Imperial finally managed to open on 9 April 1940 with a Jack Buchanan musical entertainment, *Top Hat and Tails.* It had a 36ft-deep stage and seated a substantial 1,806: 842 on the stalls floor, 514 in the dress circle, and 450 in the upper circle. (There was also basement space to shelter 275 people during air raids.) Although primarily a theatre, it incorporated projection facilities for film shows on Sundays (standard practice) – or full-time if live theatre failed. It was forced to close in June or July 1940, after losing £1,850, to await better times. The Official Receiver took over in February 1941. It then reopened as a live theatre on 1 December 1941, closed on 8 June 1942, and returned under new management on Bank Holiday Monday 3 August 1942, soon showing films on Sundays. The Imperial's first solid venture into cinema was a 'Repertory Film Season' from Sunday 15 August 1943 for several weeks. It reverted to live shows briefly before going over to films (with only very occasional live weeks) from Sunday 17 October 1943. Run by a company called Gaywood Cinemas, it obtained exclusive runs of some very minor new films such as *Prison Mutiny* and *Always a Bridesmaid* with the Andrews Sisters, but mostly showed old pictures. An excellent central location and an inviting interior enabled it to do moderately well. It also had a café.

Opposite above: The Imperial advertises 'yet another pre-release' in September 1948. An import tax dispute resulted in new Hollywood releases being withheld from the British market from August 1947, and even the town's top cinemas showed many revivals. The Imperial returned to a Christmas panto and stage shows. The situation was resolved in May 1948, whereupon a flood of new Hollywood material in excess of the requirements of the three major circuits soon became available for first run presentation. The Imperial returned to celluloid from Sunday 29 August 1948 with *Killer McCoy,* starring Mickey Rooney, 'direct from the Empire, Leicester Square' and had many more premiere runs, enabling it to proclaim a 'pre-release' policy, as it presented *The Time of Your Life, Cry of the City* and, in continuous succession, *Sleep My Love, Lulu Belle, The Black Arrow Strikes* and *The Birds and the Bees.* Such was the deluge of delayed features that even the Gaiety, normally taking late three-day runs, had a six-day Brighton premiere run of *If You Knew Susie* plus *West of the Pecos.* Of course, this abundance did not last very long.

At midnight on Thursday 8 January 1948, the world premiere of *Brighton Rock* took place at the Savoy (no other cinema was in the running, as it was made by ABC's associated production company). Cast members Hermione Baddeley, William Hartnell, Wylie Watson, Harcourt Williams and Nigel Stock, together with the director and producer, John and Roy Boulting (who, as young children, had been so impressed by the power of film at the Regent), attended a reception before the film and appeared on stage at its conclusion. Comedian Tommy Trinder was also in attendance. The film then played for two weeks at the Savoy (also concurrently, for the first week only, at ABC's Granada, Hove) amid considerable controversy over whether it was good or bad publicity for the town: faithful to Graham Greene's 1938 novel, it presented Brighton in an unfavourable light with its vivid depiction of a seedy and violent criminal underworld mingling with daytrippers.

On an earlier occasion, the Savoy used its 24-hour licence for a publicity gimmick, showing *Night and Day*, the musical biopic of Cole Porter, for twenty-four hours non-stop in 1946. When cinemas were once again allowed to turn on their external signs and neon on 2 April 1949, it became a major event. Crowds gathered, and the Savoy placed loudspeakers on the seafront canopy to catch people headed for the pier at dusk, while the Astoria called on 'Beauty and the Beast' - a pretty usherette and a monkey from the Zoo - to jointly perform the switching-on ceremony.

KING'S MINI-CINE

1a, EAST STREET, BRIGHTON

(Phone: Brighton 5918/5919).

Continuous Hourly Performance, from 12 Mid-day to 9 p.m

Spend an Hour in Warmth and Comfort.

Cartoons, Comedy, Travel. Interest, News, etc. Local News and Events

FROM TIME TO TIME.

This Week: MARCH OF THE MOVIES; BOY MEETS DOG (Cartoon); RIDE 'EM, COW-BOY; DICK WHITTINGTON'S CAT, NEWS, Etc.

Small cinemas attempted to draw audiences with programmes of news, cartoons, comedy shorts and travelogues at low prices. King's Mini-Cine opened on Friday 22 March 1946 at 1a East Street (almost opposite the Savoy's main entrance) with seventy seats, offering continuous hour-long performances on smaller gauge 16mm film from 12 noon to 9 p.m. It had previously been the Cosy Nook Theatre. The name referred to twenty-four-year-old Staff Sergeant John King of the Army Kinematograph Service (AKS), a film enthusiast since childhood, who created his first cinema in the family's garden shed. He was partnered by two ex-AKS colleagues, and hoped to secure his own early release to join them in the Brighton venture. He also planned to make sound shorts of local events to be presented exclusively at King's Mini-Cine. The bijou cinema lasted around four years. King later established Film House elsewhere in East Street as the home of John King (Films) Ltd which had a shop selling film equipment to the left of the entrance doors, and a recording studio to the right with a grand piano in the basement. King ran an extensive library of 16mm films for hire, sold 8mm and 16mm equipment (later videotapes), and at one time ran mobile cinemas that toured south east England. He established branches of his shop in London, Hove and Worthing.

The 300-seat King's Cliff (or Kingscliff) cinema at Kemp Town became the Metro News Kine in 1946 under new ownership, opening rather late at 3.15 p.m. daily. Its news theatre policy gave way to feature films and a reduction of name to just 'Metro' by the end of July 1946, followed apparently by closure on Saturday 30 November 1946. It became the Playhouse Theatre, with live repertory productions, and was taken over by Miles Byrne in October 1948. French films were introduced on Sundays when there were no stage performances. The repertory company was then dismissed and the building became the Playhouse Cinema, retaining foreign films on Sundays and opening with a six-day revival of *The Best Years of Our Lives*. It showed a mixture of films but by 1950 specialised in high-quality programming of foreign productions. To consolidate this policy, it closed for new seats and heating to be installed, and reopened as the Continental Playhouse, soon Continentale.

In August 1947, the Princes in North Street was taken over by Jacey Cinemas, a company which operated news theatres in Birmingham, Bristol and Manchester. It was relaunched on 14 October 1947 as the Princes News Theatre with 450 seats, at last establishing a successful newsreel cinema in a good location where weary shoppers were ready to pop in for an hour's relaxation.

four

The 1950s

The 1950s was a tumultuous decade for British cinemas as attendances more than halved through the impact of television, the improved comfort of home and increasing alternative forms of recreation. This had little impact on the number of cinemas in the area, forcing only the demise of two minor halls, the Arcadia, Lewes Road, and the Pavilion, Portslade-by-Sea. A third cinema, the Palladium, was compelled to close for a much-delayed major redevelopment scheme.

Hollywood fought television by making more films in colour and setting off a short-lived wave of films in three dimensions. It also became more daring in subject matter, as did Continental film makers. An 'X' certificate was introduced by the British Board of Film Censors, restricting entry to those over sixteen years of age. The censor's certificates were merely advisory, but local authorities usually accepted them. By the end of the year the Odeon, West Street and ABC's Savoy and Granada had shown 'X' films from Hollywood – *Detective Story* and *Murder Inc.* respectively. But the Odeon and Gaumont chains showed as few 'X's as possible, because they prevented family attendance. The ABC circuit was much more welcoming, but when it gave a national release in 1952 to a British drama, *Cosh Boy*, this was banned by Hove in case it influenced teenage behaviour. However, Hove permitted a banned American 'B' film, *Wicked Woman*, which allowed the Rothbury to stage its two-week Sussex premiere as a main feature attraction. Later in the decade, *Rock Around the Clock* had been shown without fuss in August 1956 at the Regent before disorderly behaviour elsewhere claimed national headlines. Brighton Council took no chances and banned any further screenings.

By 1950, foreign films were being widely shown, usually paired with English language productions to reduce the strain of reading subtitles (although some Continental pictures were expertly dubbed into English). There was competition for some of the top foreign attractions: the Astoria played the 'X' certificate *Le Plaisir* concurrently with the Curzon, although the drama *Bicycle Thieves* played first at the Astoria and only later at the Curzon. Many foreign films also appeared at the Palladium. The major circuits played some highly-praised French films, including two thrillers, *The Wages of Fear* and *The Fiends*, Jacques Tati's comedy *My Uncle,* and the colourful *French Can Can* - partly to test their appeal, partly to alleviate a film shortage as Hollywood cut back on production.

The Coronation of Queen Elizabeth II on Tuesday 2 June 1953 was a milestone for both cinema and television, the biggest assignment ever undertaken by British newsreels and the BBC's biggest outside broadcast to date. Television could only show it in black and white, but millions were won over to the medium by its live coverage. Brighton cinemas showed short reels of the drive from Buckingham Palace to Westminster Abbey later the same day, after they were flown to Shoreham airport. The following day, and again by air, a newsreel containing the actual Abbey ceremony arrived at the Regent, Odeon, Academy and Curzon. The Savoy was first with a full film record, *Elizabeth Is Queen* in WarnerColor, from Saturday 6 June (the Granada followed a day later), and this went into the Embassy on Thursday 11 June and into the Curzon and Rothbury the following week. *A Queen Is Crowned*, the full-length Technicolor documentary that was the biggest box-office attraction of the year, played at both the Odeon and Regent four times daily from Sunday 7 June for a week, then two weeks later went into the Academy and the Odeons at Hove and Kemp Town, reflecting their second-run status (the three cinemas often played in tandem at this period), subsequently arriving at the Gaiety for three days from 5 July. The Rothbury and Gaiety had both played the short *Coronation Day* in Gevacolor from Monday 8 June, when the Princes advertised a 'full length' Coronation film of unidentified title. Other cinemas tried counter-programming for those bored by the Royal frolics.

From early days, inventors had tried to add depth to the screen. The Arcadia in February 1914 had dabbled with its own invention of the stereoscopograph, and the Regent tried showing 3D films without the use of special viewing glasses in 1925. However, 3D really arrived in 1953 and, to achieve the full effect, two interlocked prints were projected simultaneously onto a special treated screen. Even with enlarged spools, there had to be an interval halfway through to reload the projectors. 3D proved a very profitable gimmick, but the poor quality of many films, complaints of headaches and eye strain, and the arrival of CinemaScope combined to kill it off.

The wide screen era began when a number of cinemas installed new 'panoramic' or 'giant' screens. A bigger image was projected onto a wider screen – which was fine for new films shot with this in mind, but it meant that the top and bottom of older pictures were crudely cut off. It was ill-advised of late-run cinemas like the Rothbury, Portslade, and the Gaiety, Lewes Road, to install them before they could play many suitable films. In any case, these screens had to be replaced by even wider ones with variable masking that could open out for films in CinemaScope where the picture was about two and a half times wider than it was tall. The novelty of CinemaScope wore off, but the Essoldo (ex-Imperial) in particular used it to draw huge audiences for a while.

Like other top seaside resorts, Brighton played many new films during the season concurrently with, or very soon after, the West End. The Odeon, Regent and Savoy started new programmes on Thursdays so that holidaymakers staying for a calendar week or fortnight had more new films from which to choose. Brighton also became one of the towns to introduce exclusive extended runs aimed not only at holidaymakers but also at the hinterland where cinemagoers would wait years for the same films to appear locally. Occasional regular release films – like the early CinemaScope attractions and *Reach for the Sky* and *Some Like It Hot* – had first runs of two weeks or even three, but the big change commenced in the summer of 1958 when *Around the World in 80 Days* played at the Odeon, West Street, continuously at normal prices for four weeks. The 'roadshow' era really got underway with the almost simultaneous openings of *South Pacific* in the Astoria (which was fitted out with a huge, deeply curved screen for the Todd AO process, akin to Cinerama but without the joins) and *The Ten Commandments* at the Academy. 'Hard ticket' runs gave both these secondary halls a new lease of life, especially the Astoria.

Brighton Cinima attractions for 16 May 1950 (courtesy of Keith Skone).

In April 1949, the Imperial was taken over for 'a very high figure' by the Newcastle-based Essoldo circuit ('Essoldo' was derived from the first names of the circuit founder, Sol Sheckman, his wife Esther and his daughter Dorothy). The Imperial immediately advertised itself as 'An Essoldo Theatre', and then took the circuit name from Sunday 7 May 1950. The double-bill of *Bomba, The Jungle Boy* and *Brimstone* from the following day was rather typical of the poor material the cinema could then obtain. *711 Ocean Drive*, the main feature advertised in the above photograph (from the Brighton History Centre, Brighton Museum) was another lesser release receiving its first showing in Brighton in early 1951. The Essoldo chain grew to be the fourth largest in the country, after ABC, Gaumont and Odeon. The lettering in Brighton, with red neon, was not in the distinctive circuit style with two stretched letter 'S''s, although this was used in press advertising.

Despite its prominent position in North Street, the Essoldo must have been hard-pressed to fill its 1,877 seats when superior first-run attractions were usually playing at the adjacent Regent and nearby Odeon and Savoy. The Essoldo was principally in competition with the Astoria for the films the big circuits didn't take, although occasionally they would agree to a concurrent booking, as when both played *Tarzan's Magic Fountain* in 1951. In February of the same year, the Essoldo played *Manon*, the first 'X' certificate film in Brighton. Previously banned, this French festival award winner, starring seventeen-year-old Cécile Aubry, was viewed by Brighton's Watch Committee and passed for screening. Thanks to the controversy, it ran for two weeks. Exploitation films dressed as sex education were always applying for local certificates and *Should Parents Tell?*, about a girl whose parents didn't tell her the facts of life, was viewed by the Brighton Watch Committee and approved for showing at the Essoldo in October–November 1950 to adults only.

THE ESSOLDO

TEL 22211 · NORTH ST. BRIGHTON

COMMENCING SUNDAY, JUNE 14th

First Full Length 3-D in Brighton
AUDREY TOTTER   EDMOND O'BRIEN
MAN IN THE DARK
Cleo Moore   Hugo Haas   ONE GIRL'S CONFESSION   (a)
PLEASE NOTE — SEPARATE PERFORMANCES
Doors 12.30 Commence 1.0   Doors 4.0 Commence 4.15   Doors 7.15 Commence 7.45
PRICES OF ADMISSION: 2/6   3/3   3/9   4/1

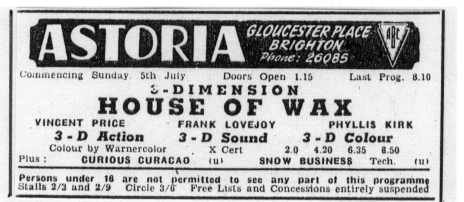

ASTORIA   GLOUCESTER PLACE   BRIGHTON   ABC   Phone: 26085

Commencing Sunday. 5th July   Doors Open 1.15   Last Prog. 8.10

3-DIMENSION
HOUSE OF WAX
VINCENT PRICE   FRANK LOVEJOY   PHYLLIS KIRK
3 - D Action   3 - D Sound   3 - D Colour
Colour by Warnercolor   X Cert   2.0   4.20   6.35   8.50
Plus :   CURIOUS CURACAO   (u)   SNOW BUSINESS   Tech.   (u)

Persons under 16 are not permitted to see any part of this programme
Stalls 2/3 and 2/9   Circle 3/6   Free Lists and Concessions entirely suspended

Interest in 3D films was revived by the huge popularity of shorts shown at the Festival of Britain in 1951. The Curzon brought some of these films to Brighton for special morning showings at sixpence during the week of 6 April 1952. A form of 3D had been used for a short time in the 1930s, and an old Hollywood short, *Metroscopix*, was revived in support of the western *The Naked Spur* at the Savoy and Granada for a week from Thursday 2 April 1953.

Hollywood produced new 3D feature films that could only be shown in specially equipped cinemas. As always desperate for big attractions, the large Essoldo and Astoria jumped at the opportunity. The Essoldo got in first with a mediocre thriller called *Man in the Dark* from Sunday 14 June 1953, followed immediately by a week of the equally undistinguished *Bwana Devil*, the first full-length 3D film made, both shown three times daily in separate performances at increased prices. However, it was the Astoria that really scored with 3D when it opened *House of Wax* on Sunday 5 July 1953 with four performances on weekdays. A smash hit in London, this 'X' certificate horror film also had Technicolor; it delivered real chills and thrills and played for four weeks, matching the run of *Gone with the Wind* in 1942 but with twice as many screenings. It was followed by a 3D jungle adventure, *Sangaree*, on the Astoria's 'New Giant Panoramic Screen', the first wide screen in Brighton. Later, the Astoria staged the British premiere of a minor 3D Hollywood shocker, *The Maze*. (These films could also be shown 'flat'. When the Palladium booked *House of Wax* in May 1954, it advised 'Not 3D' in small print. The film returned in 3D in 1961 to scare a new generation at the Essoldo.)

During the first half of 1954, the ABC circuit equipped most of its leading cinemas to present films in 3D, including *Phantom of the Rue Morgue, Kiss Me Kate* and *Hondo*, but they were all shown 'flat' at the Savoy and Granada. So rigid was film-booking that the Astoria could only play them – 'first time in 3D' – a few weeks later.

Above: CinemaScope reached Brighton on Monday 11 January 1954 when the first film to be released in the process, *The Robe*, opened at the Odeon, West Street, with full stereophonic sound. The Biblical epic had a three-week run, initially shown five times daily (from 10 a.m.!), then reduced to four screenings, all at normal prices. This Odeon was one of the first eight on the circuit to show *The Robe* after its West End opening, along with the Odeons at Birmingham, Glasgow, Leeds, Liverpool, Manchester and Newcastle and the Capitol, Cardiff. Installation was an expensive business (an estimated £8,000 in Brighton) as, at this time, all the screens had to be flown in from America. These needed to be installed further forward than the old screen to be fully visible to cinemagoers sitting on the sides of the auditorium. At Brighton, forty-six seats were removed for being too close to the screen for comfort. The screen curtains, with their winged horse and charioteer, became the main curtains at the Academy, used until its closure in 1973.

No further CinemaScope films played at the Odeon during 1954, because 20th Century-Fox, the studio promoting CinemaScope, stopped supplying the Odeon and Gaumont circuits after they refused to put in stereophonic sound and agree to extended runs at every cinema. Fox formed a new alliance with smaller chains which were happy to meet its demands. This brought about the Essoldo's most successful period as a cinema, beginning with Fox's second release in CinemaScope, the comedy *How To Marry a Millionaire*, which ran for two weeks in North Street from 1 March with full stereophonic sound. The Essoldo showed a dozen Fox films in 1954 for two weeks or more (some with supporting CinemaScope shorts), including *Three Coins in the Fountain* and *Long John Silver*, both concurrent with London's West End, and the Royal Tour documentary *Flight of the White Heron*, which played for three weeks and then returned for a fourth. The Essoldo also revived *The Robe* for a week. (Between CinemaScope films, it fell back on low-grade rubbish and the occasional live booking.)

CinemaScope films were being made by other Hollywood studios. The Warner Bros. western *The Command* played in the process at the Savoy and Granada in July 1954 and at the Astoria in August. Other early 'scope films screened at all three ABC cinemas included Metro-Goldwyn-Mayer's British-made *Knights of the Round Table* and the Warner musical *Lucky Me*. There was no mention of stereophonic sound. CinemaScope was very disappointing at the Savoy as it looked too small and 'letterboxed', wedged in the thirty-four foot opening. The new screen at the Astoria replaced its 3D one. The Odeon West Street's second CinemaScope presentation, *Sign of the Pagan*, was a Universal picture handled by Rank through General Film Distributors. It opened on 2 January 1955 with full stereophonic sound.

The Randolph Richards circuit enthusiastically embraced the process and, by early December 1954, the Gaiety, Lewes Road, had CinemaScope with full stereophonic sound, even though it had to play the Fox films after the larger and more central Essoldo. The Gaiety became the third Brighton cinema to present *The Robe* (for a week at Christmas) and one of the first in the country to play other Fox CinemaScope films for only three days.

Below: The new CinemaScope screen at the Gaiety, Lewes Road, which initially advertised 'CinemaScope in its entirety', presumably referring to stereophonic sound. (Taken from the Chris Horlock collection.)

Opposite: This page of Brighton entertainments in May 1955 is arranged alphabetically.

The Regent is reopening after 'extensive reconstruction' caused by fitting CinemaScope. The curving front of the balcony obstructed the wider projection beam. Work started outside opening hours at the end of February, then the Regent closed from Thursday 14 April to Wednesday 18 May for the balcony to be cut back and a new screen installed. One of the two films on the reopening double bill is in CinemaScope: the Victor Mature western *Valley of Fury*. An earlier CinemaScope film, *The Black Shield of Falworth*, had played at the Regent (and subsequently at the Academy) in one of the alternative, non-'scope versions that were briefly available. Note the highlighting of CinemaScope films at the Essoldo, Gaiety, Granada and Savoy. The VistaVision process advertised at the Odeon, Brighton, for *Run for Cover* was not a 'scope system but gave improved picture quality.

Of course, the novelty of CinemaScope soon wore off, but every cinema had to install it to stay in business. The Duke of York's had far too narrow a proscenium arch to fit CinemaScope. Local architects Thomas Garrett & Son drew up plans for a new 32ft-wide proscenium arch to contain a screen 28ft wide by 12ft high, almost twice as wide as the old one, with seating reduced to 750. Work was done in the mornings and overnight from Wednesday 8 December 1955 to avoid closing the cinema. The new arch, lit at the sides and top by concealed lighting and decorated with stars, remains to this day. CinemaScope made its bow on Monday 6 February 1956 with a three-day booking of *The Student Prince*, so successful that the musical returned for a further three-day run on Thursday 1 March (and again in May 1960, and for an afternoon show in January 1977). Despite this major improvement, the Duke of York's remained at the end of the line for new releases.

The Paris is a new addition to the film scene – or rather, the former Court under a new name. Since 1947, the building had been leased by J. Baxter Somerville who returned it to live theatre use, first as the Dolphin and then as Her Majesty's. Lewis Cohen, chairman of the non-profit company which owned the theatre, as well as the almost adjacent Theatre Royal, concluded that there wasn't room for both and drew up a plan to sell off Her Majesty's for replacement by offices and shops, using the proceeds to improve the Theatre Royal. Somerville was furiously opposed to the destruction of his theatre, refused to give up his lease, and used his own money to convert it back into a cinema in association with George Fernie, owner of the Continentale cinema at Kemp Town. The gala reopening as the Paris took place on Wednesday 6 April 1955 with a two-week run of the saucy Fernandel comedy *The Sheep Has Five Legs* (which returned for a third week later). Besides *Seven Samurai,* the Paris also showed *Monsieur Hulot's Holiday*, setting high standards as the town's new outlet for foreign films. The partnership with Mr Fernie was terminated in July 1958, leaving Mr Somerville in charge.

SATURDAY SHOWS

ACADEMY: Dale Robertson in Top of the World (A) at 2.25, 5.40, 9.0; Canyon Crossroads (U).

ASTORIA: Eva Stiberg in Unmarried Mothers (X) at 2.30, 5.40, 8.50; Hands of Destiny (U).

CONTINENTALE: Georges Marchal in Fatale Affaire (A) at 2.0, 5.20, 8.40; Boîte De Nuit (A).

CURZON: Animal Farm (U) at 2.55, 6.0, 9.10; Laughter in Paradise (U).

EMBASSY: Ray Milland in Something to Live For (A) at 2.40, 5.50, 9.0; Crosswinds (A).

ESSOLDO: Jean Simmons in The Egyptian (A) at 1.50, 4.50, 7.50.

GAIETY: Dirk Bogarde in Simba (A) at 2.45, 5.50, 8.55; Secret Venture (U).

GRANADA: Rex Harrison in The Constant Husband (U) at 2.15, 5.50, 8.55; Security Risk (A).

HIPPODROME: Evelyn Laye in Wedding in Paris (A) at 2.30 and 7.30.

ODEON, BRIGHTON: Alec Guinness in The Prisoner (A) at 2.20, 5.40, 8.55; The Black Dakotas (U).

ODEON, HOVE: Jack Buchanan in As Long As They're Happy (U) at 2.45, 5.40, 8.10; On the Barrier Reef (U).

ODEON, KEMP TOWN: Tyrone Power in The Long Gray Line at 2.30, 4.15, 8.10; Sky Commando (U).

PALACE PIER: The Dashing White Sergeant at 5.0 and 7.45.

PALLADIUM: Barbara Stanwyck in Witness to Murder (A) at 2.55, 6.0 and 9.5; The Diamond (A).

PARIS: Akira Kurosawa's Seven Samurai (X) at 1.55, 4.50, 7.50.

PRINCES NEWS: Crazy Week film "shorts" (daily from 10.30).

ROTHBURY: John Wayne in She Wore A Yellow Ribbon at 1.50, 5.10, 8.40; The Scarlet Spear (U).

SAVOY: Judy Garland in A Star Is Born (A) at 1.15, 4.30, 7.45.

THEATRE ROYAL: Betty Ann Davies in Witness for the Prosecution at 2.30 and 7.45.

Gene Tierney plays a princess with ideas, in "The Egyptian" at the Essoldo Cinema, Brighton, this week.

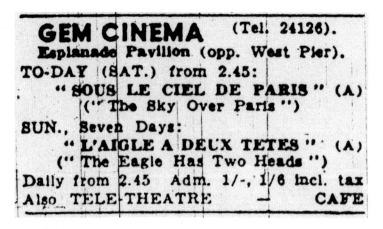

GEM CINEMA (Tel. 24126).
Esplanade Pavilion (opp. West Pier).
TO-DAY (SAT.) from 2.45:
 " SOUS LE CIEL DE PARIS " (A)
 (" The Sky Over Paris ")
SUN., Seven Days:
 " L'AIGLE A DEUX TETES " (A)
 (" The Eagle Has Two Heads ")
Daily from 2.45 Adm. 1/-, 1/6 incl. tax
Also TELE-THEATRE — CAFE

Above: Against the trend to bigger screens came a most unlikely venture. Brighton's second cinema to be called the Gem opened quietly on Wednesday 29 September 1954 in the Esplandade Pavilion opposite the West Pier. The address, 132 Kings Road, was the same as that of the Pandora Gallery, the town's very first cinema in 1896. The Gem started off reviving foreign and British films ('Good Films You May Have Missed') and then homed in on sixty-minute shows of silent comedy changed six times a fortnight, even advertising live guest stars (no names). It called itself 'Britain's Smallest Cinema' and certainly took the smallest newspaper advertisements, away from the regular film section where it was never listed. The Gem became a live theatre on 1 September 1955 when the Old Time Film Season, now changed weekly, was relegated to afternoons and Sundays. It was advertising Valentino in *Son of the Sheik* in October 1955, but then seems to vanish from sight.

Opposite above: the Palladium on Brighton's seafront had remained a profitable cinema, thanks to its location and low prices (still opening as early as 11.15am on Sunday and Monday). The theatre was compulsorily taken over for a major redevelopment scheme, and its operator, M. Blok (or Bloch - the Brighton exhibitor of First World War days?), received £4,200 compensation from Brighton Corporation for the remaining seventeen years of his lease. The last programme was a sure-fire revival double bill of *Genevieve* and *Doctor in the House* for the seven days ending Saturday 26 May 1956.

Another cinema closed on the same day. Although the Arcadia, Lewes Road, had advertised *On the Carpet*, a reissue of a 1946 Abbott and Costello comedy, patrons found a sign on the doors: 'Closed until further notice'. Dennis Williams recalls: 'The auditorium was very bleak and devoid of decoration. Although the Arcadia never enjoyed a good reputation, the seating was very good and the projection and sound excellent.' There were plans to turn the building into a variety and concert hall with occasional 16mm film shows and trade exhibitions under the name Advershowdrome, but the auditorium was eventually demolished for the Brighton Trades Union and Labour Club to be built. This made use of the foyer and passage to the cinema, until these too were replaced and nothing remained of the cinema.

The Pavilion at Portslade was the third local cinema to close during the 1950s, after a three-day run of *The Lonely Man* plus *Scared Stiff* to Saturday 15 February 1958. Shortly before, it seems to have featured in local filming of the war drama *The Battle of the V.1* starring Michael Rennie and Patricia Medina. The seats and some of the carpet went to the Rex (ex-Cinema de Luxe) at Newhaven. The Pavilion name sign lingered at the top of the façade after the building was converted to industrial use and the foyer removed to provide vehicle access to the former auditorium. It still stands as the premises of London and Brighton Plating.

The Palladium, closed and awaiting demolition. The rear of the auditorium is seen up the short passage to the right of the entrance, with the projection box high up. (Both pictures courtesy of Chris Horlock.) The building, with its wonderful Frank Matcham auditorium still intact, was finally destroyed in 1963 to make way for part of the Brighton Conference Centre. (In 1960 and 1961, the Palladium name was adopted by the S.S. Brighton in West Street for its Christmas pantomime on ice, along with wrestling and ice-skating.)

Right: This mid-1956 photograph shows the Savoy, Brighton, with one of the large triangular signs erected on most ABC cinemas after the Second World War to establish a stronger circuit identity. The Savoy name was in white with green neon, the rest in red and blue reinforced by neon. The Astoria received a similar sign.

Below: On 28 March 1957 the Regent, Brighton, hosts a charity county premiere of the British comedy *Doctor at Large*. The two-week public run followed on 18 April. Donald Sinden, Muriel Pavlow, Derek Farr and the parents of principal star Dirk Bogarde attended. This view (courtesy of Brighton History Centre, Brighton Museum) shows the later canopy design with illuminated lettering on the front edge reading REGENT THEATRE BALLROOM RESTAURANT REGENT and the V-shaped display of the current programme on top.

The Savoy as modernised in 1958. Despite the national decline in attendances, the major cinemas were still very profitable, and the ABC circuit decided to completely modernise the interior of the Savoy, doing away with what was left of its faded and outdated oriental decorative scheme. The Savoy closed on 5 February 1958, to be reopened by the Mayor on 27 March with a special showing of the Marlon Brando picture *Sayonara* and personal appearances by two stars, Janette Scott and John Fraser, who were not in the film but under contract to ABC's associated production company based at Elstree Studios. The Fanfare Trumpeters from the Central Band of the RAF also performed, plus Peter Kilby at the Hammond Electronic Organ imported for the occasion (the original organ console had just been removed). The much larger new wide screen with two sets of tabs was installed in front of the old screen (which was left in position). The Savoy lost 214 seats from the front stalls but retained a massive total of 2,304. It continued to operate a café (modernised into more of a coffee bar) and dance hall. This view was taken in 1975 by John Fernee, just before the auditorium was carved up into four cinemas.

The Astoria, Brighton, as modernised in 1958 (photographs by John Fernee, taken 1975).

★ ★ ★ ★ ★ ★ ★ ★ ★ ★ ★ ★ ★

**NOW! Exclusive to
Kent and Sussex**
BREATHTAKING
TODD-AO!

RODGERS and HAMMERSTEIN'S

SOUTH PACIFIC

'U'

Produced by BOBBY **ADLER** · Directed by JOSHUA L **LOGAN**

Starring ROSSANO **BRAZZI** · MITZI **GAYNOR** · DON **KERR**

Screenplay by PAUL OSBORN featuring RAY WALSTON presents in **Technicolor**
Produced at 20th CENTURY-FOX
Distributed by 20th CENTURY-FOX
A SOUTH PACIFIC ENTERPRISES INC. PRODUCTION

Commencing TODAY at 6.45 p.m.

ABC ASTORIA - Brighton
PHONE 26085
TWO SEPARATE PERFORMANCES DAILY
PETER KILBY entertains at the Electronic Organ
Afternoons at 1.30 p.m.   Evenings at 6.45 p.m.
FILM PROGRAMME COMMENCES
Afternoons at 2.30 p.m.   Evenings at 7.45 p.m.
PRICES, incl. tax: Stalls 3/-, 5/-; Circle: 6/6, 7/6
ALL SEATS MAY BE BOOKED IN ADVANCE

ADVANCE BOOKING OFFICE OPEN AT THE ASTORIA 10 a.m to 8 p.m

**TONIGHT
GALA CIVIC OPENING**
in the presence of
His Worship the Mayor of Brighton
(Councillor A. J. Sadler, J.P.)

The Astoria was struggling to survive on revivals of old hits like *High Noon* and *The African Queen* and weak new releases when ABC decided to test the idea of establishing 'roadshow houses' for extended runs outside London's West End. The Astoria was refitted at a cost of £20,000 with a 50ft by 27ft curved screen and Todd-A0 (70mm) projection equipment in a new, lower box at the back of the circle to provide a better angle of throw. The side walls were covered in drapes and the back wall of the stalls was brought forward to the point where the taller screen could be fully seen, reducing overall seating to 1,200. This also marked the end of occasional live shows.

The Astoria was relaunched on 2 August 1958 with *South Pacific*, which had opened in London in April. Its run in Brighton until Saturday 10 January 1959 was by far the longest of any film to that date in the town. An electronic organ was regularly played before the film by Peter Kilby, with occasional weeks taken over by Reginald Porter-Brown. This made the show a partially live one, which significantly reduced the amount of entertainments tax that had to be paid. After *South Pacific* (which had a further engagement from April 1960), the Astoria returned to its former policy of revivals and trashy 'exploitation' fare like *Nudist Paradise*. It continued to hold ABC Minors shows on Saturday mornings. Then it became one of the first three cinemas outside London to play the hit musical *Gigi* (in 35mm CinemaScope) - from Sunday 1 March to 30 May 1959 and again from Monday 27 July to 31 October 1959 (matinees only on Wednesdays and weekends). The next extended run was *The Nun's Story* from Sunday 13 December, again with Peter Kilby at the electronic organ. Until June 1962, the Astoria, Brighton, was the only cinema in Sussex able to show 70mm films and it had the pick of the new attractions released in the format. However, rival roadshow engagements using regular 35mm prints began the day after the Astoria launched *South Pacific,* when the Academy presented *The Ten Commandments* at increased prices but with continuous performances starting at 10.15 a.m. on Mondays to Saturdays - the evening and the two Sunday shows being bookable in advance. The biblical epic ran until 13 September 1958, and then returned from 31 May 1959 to 27 June 1959.

This summer 1958 photograph (courtesy of Chris Horlock) shows on the left the secondary entrance to the Regent, with the Essoldo beyond. The Essoldo was built later (as the Imperial) and was set further back to widen North Road. The narrow Windsor Street is between them, visible through the open Regent foyer. 20th Century-Fox had recently resolved its dispute with the Odeon and Gaumont chains in order to obtain a wider release for its films, and the third of its new CinemaScope pictures to play the Gaumont circuit, an 'X' certificate semi-horror western *The Fiend Who Walked the West*, is showing at the Regent. This would have otherwise appeared at the Essoldo, which faced increasing booking difficulties that led to the eventual end of films. It was still used for live shows from time to time: both the Royal Ballet and Ballet Rambert appeared for a week in 1958/59. In 1960 there was even a play starring Donald Wolfit in June as well as a further visit from the Ballet Rambert the following week and a seven-week summer show starring Cyril Fletcher (with films on Sundays).

five

The 1960s

During the 1960s, the film business changed drastically. Attendances nationally fell from 500 million per year in 1960 to 215 million in 1969. Audiences flocked to the few hit films and shunned the rest unless they offered sex or violence.

The Savoy and Granada, Hove (both renamed ABC) and the Odeon took the pick of the regular releases, playing the best, like the James Bond film *Goldfinger*, for two or more weeks. The Astoria and the Regent took the pick of the roadshows. The Academy extended the run of some roadshows and initiated a few of its own. In line with its advertising slogan ('Famous for Famous Films'), the Curzon continued its policy of playing and replaying recent hits (it had *Goldfinger* back every two or three months in 1965). The Embassy, the Duke of York's and the Gaiety (which became the Ace) adopted a similar policy. Alternatives to showing films were explored by cinema owners. The Odeon, Hove, closed on 18 February 1961 only because its vast sloping floor made it ideal for conversion into the second Top Rank ten-pin bowling alley, opened in July 1961. However, a rival AMF bowl called the King Alfred Lanes opened first, and two bowling alleys in Hove proved one - if not two - too many. Bowling proved a huge disappointment in this country and the former Odeon building was sold in 1969, being demolished the following year. Its site is occupied by shops and offices, including Autocentre and Tesco Express in 2003.

Then there was bingo. This required relatively minor alterations and had the advantage of being a fixed attraction that could draw regular attendance from a much smaller number of patrons. It was established at the Ritz in West Street (formerly Sherry's dance hall) in March 1961 and at the Regent ballroom on Monday evenings and Wednesday afternoons from early May 1961, and from January 1962 it was successfully introduced at the disused Odeon, Kemp Town (closed on Saturday 5 November 1960 because it was losing too much money).

Next to succumb was the Rothbury at Portslade. It ran a pair of old films, *Green Fire* and *Ride, Vaquero*, for three days to Saturday 18 January 1964, then played two even older films, *Champion* and *Where Danger Lives* the following day (teenagers made Sunday opening profitable). It went over to Mecca bingo nightly from Thursday 23 January 1964, and failed *c.* 1978, unable to compete with the club established in the former Granada/ABC, Hove. It has since become home to a local radio station (currently Southern FM) with all signs of its cinema past long removed.

Later in 1964, the Essoldo caved in. It had soldiered on with every naturist feature going; wrestling on Thursdays; one-night pop concerts with Cliff Richard, Brenda Lee and Gene Vincent, Billy Fury, Jerry Lee Lewis, Bobby Vee and the Crickets, Adam Faith, Freddie and the Dreamers and others; stage productions like *Doctor in the House* and *Billy Liar;* Shakespeare from the Old Vic company and musicals by the Brighton and Hove Operatic Society. After a week's run of two dubbed costume pictures, *Jason and the Golden Fleece* and *Invasion of the Normans*, it closed with a Sunday 10 May booking of *Never Let Go* and *Teenage Lovers*. Joe Brown had performed the last concert on 27 March. Essoldo started its own bingo operation from Friday 15 May. The hall was no longer available for one-night concerts or one-week live shows for fear of losing its bingo regulars: they alone enjoyed the building for the next thirty years. There was a further defection to bingo in 1968 by the Ace (ex-Gaiety), Lewes Road. The Duke of York's sought the best of both worlds by introducing bingo on Fridays and Tuesdays from 12 March 1965, but full-time cinema resumed on Wednesday 1 July 1970.

The most important development in the local cinema scene occurred when the British Film Institute decided that Brighton should have its own version of London's National Film Theatre. The Brighton Film Theatre opened in 1969 with a quite remarkable range of programming.

The 1960s was the Astoria's finest decade as it thrived on its 'roadshow' policy of extended runs. *Ben-Hur* opened on Sunday 26 March 1961 (more than a year after its West End premiere). Although the Rank-owned Regent got into the act by taking *The Guns of Navarone* for a seven-week season from 18 May 1961, the Astoria retained exclusive access to films available on 70mm and Rank's own distribution company supplied two major epics, *Spartacus* and *El Cid*, for lengthy runs.

To resolve this unsatisfactory situation, Rank closed the Regent on Wednesday 25 April 1962 to install 70mm and a much larger screen within a very plain proscenium arch that replaced the one dating from 1929. It reopened on Thursday 7 June with a five-week run of *Barabbas*, then returned to regular circuit weekly releases until opening *Der Rosenkavalier* and *The Longest Day*. The biggest special presentation of this period was the Astoria's *West Side Story*, which ran for twenty-one weeks from 10 June until 20 October 1962. In 1963, it was *Lawrence of Arabia* at the Regent that scored the best, running from 30 May to 9 October.

The longest uninterrupted run of any film in Brighton commenced on Thursday 15 April 1965 at the Regent. *The Sound of Music* initially ran for more than a year, to Wednesday 25 May 1966. It transferred after a three-day gap to the Academy for nearly five months, to Saturday 15 October 1966. It was then back at the Regent from Thursday 20 October to 23 November 1966. (The gaps reflect the different start days of the two cinemas.) The film returned to the Academy on 19 December 1968 and was frequently shown at other cinemas, including the Curzon and the Ace, filtering down to the Duke of York's for an exceptional two-week run. In 1965, there was a real battle between musicals. *Mary Poppins* opened at the Odeon on the same day as *The Sound of Music* but with continuous performances at increased prices. Three days later, the Astoria commenced its run of *My Fair Lady*, which lasted until 24 December 1965.

On 23 June 1966 the Astoria became the first cinema to show *Doctor Zhivago* after the West End. It ran until to 3 May 1967, returning later in the year from 10 August to 25 October. It also played at the Regent in 1968. Although *2001: A Space Odyssey* was initially released to Cinerama theatres in the summer of 1968, it also opened in 70mm at the Astoria when, it is reputed, the manager went into hiding to avoid trying to explain what the film was about. The last year of the decade saw the Regent offering such titles as *Funny Girl*, *Oliver!* and *Battle of Britain* while the Astoria responded with *Where Eagles Dare*, *Mayerling*, *Ice Station Zebra*, etc.

Above: On 26 April 1961 the Savoy was renamed the ABC as part of a general rebranding to give the circuit a stronger identity. The large, attractive triangular sign with its neon was replaced on both entrances by a dreary vertical sign with four internally-lit lozenge-shaped boxes, the last of which featured the old triangle sign in miniature. The main East Street frontage is seen in January 1967, with a backlit 'readagraph' display of the current programme having replaced the old overhanging canopy. ABC put in an outline planning application in early 1963 to replace the seafront entrance with eight flats over ground floor shops (the scheme never happened).

Left: The Astoria still has its triangle sign in 1964, advertising a six-day booking between roadshows.

Major internal alterations were carried out at the Granada, Hove, following the extensive changes to the ABC circuit's two cinemas in Brighton, the Savoy/ABC and Astoria, and the closure of the other cinema in Hove, the Odeon, on 18 February 1961 for conversion to a bowling alley. For the past few years, the Odeon had been upgraded to show films almost simultaneously with the Odeon, West Street, matching the Granada's policy of starting three days after the Savoy/ABC. The Odeon, Hove's, last attraction was *The Singer Not the Song*, starring Dirk Bogarde and John Mills, plus a travelogue, *Japan*.

With the Odeon gone, the Granada mixed the best of the Odeon releases with its own ABC programmes. It was the only ABC cinema on the South Coast able to tap into its rival's top attractions in this way. This encouraged a thorough redecoration and modernisation, starting 26 December 1962, resulting in a new low ceiling in the foyer, respacing of the stalls (losing 200 seats) and additional carpet on the floors.

In this June 1965 photograph, the Granada has just been renamed the ABC (the change took effect on 27 May 1965). The old triangle trademark was retained in the lowest of the four 'lozenges' until EMI took over the circuit in 1969 and inserted its name instead. Here, the ABC is showing the CinemaScope general release version of *How The West Was Won*, the three-panel Cinerama production that had its world premiere in London in November 1962.

The Paris, shortly after closing on Saturday 2 March 1963. The Buttery advertised on the sign was a basement bar (Courtesy of Chris Horlock).

The Paris closed with a totally uncharacteristic week's run of two Hollywood musicals, *Carousel* and *Carmen Jones*. The previous week's Ingmar Bergman comedy *The Devil's Eye* plus Israeli film *They Were Ten* reflected the usual policy of showing worthwhile foreign films. In fact, Bergman's output had been a regular attraction over the years. (At one time, it had operated a Gala Film Club on Sundays, showing mostly important films banned or cut by the censor.) Sadly, the Paris's enterprise had not been rewarded. Perhaps it was too large with 600 seats, but manageress Anne Travers reported: 'I myself have acted as cashier, usherette and have sold ices, etc. all to try to keep losses down.' The end followed the death of lessee J. Baxter Somerville in January. Miss Travers commented: 'It was solely due to Mr Somerville's enthusiasm and love of the Paris that it has kept going as long as it has.' The executors of Mr Somerville's estate ordered it to close.

In January 1958, developers had sought to buy the site, but Mr Somerville, who had introduced foreign films to keep the theatre going in 1955, refused to give way. A campaign to save the theatre attracted the support of Laurence Olivier, Ralph Richardson, Charles Laughton and J. B. Priestley, who declared it 'the loveliest theatre I have seen on the South Coast'. The building reverted to its landlords, the adjacent Theatre Royal. It is difficult to see how the Paris could have reopened as a live theatre at that time, when even the Hippodrome was temporarily dark for lack of suitable shows. Permission was granted for offices and the Paris was demolished. Lewis Cohen, managing director of the Theatre Royal, maintained that the £70,000 received for the Paris ensured the survival of its neighbour, but only a developer could look at the bland office block at 17-19 New Road and not regret the loss of the theatre that once stood there. At least the Continentale at Kemp Town, now with just 267 seats, gave Brighton premiere runs to outstanding foreign films like *Jules and Jim* and *L'Eclisse* in between bookings of soft porn like *My Bare Lady* and Hollywood films at holiday times.

A novelty that recalled the cinema's early days as part of touring fairgrounds was the visit in May 1964 of the world's first Cinerama Mobile Theatre to Hove with 'the largest screen in the country!' This revived the very first Cinerama feature, first seen in London ten years earlier, in a large blue tent, with a conventional type of screen rather than the slatted one unique to the system (which had been designed to reduce reflection across the deep curve). Hove was the second town on a tour that extended along the South Coast, heavily promoted by posters and hanging cards as though a circus had arrived in town. Later tours of other early Cinerama features in 1965 and 1966 seem to have omitted the Brighton area.

The Princes News Theatre, seen in February 1966 (courtesy of Brighton History Centre, Brighton Museum), had relied on cartoons since newsreels had folded. It was still opening daily at 12.30 p.m., and here it includes the serial *Jesse James Rides Again* in an attempt to encourage regular attendances. The Princes had been expected to switch over to continental films when the Court closed - but the Court had been losing money with them and the cartoon policy was still profitable. However, the supply of cartoons was drying up and the owners, Jacey Cinemas, were switching their newsreel theatres elsewhere to foreign films. After Thursday 14 April 1966, the Brighton cinema closed for two days of 'technical alterations' (principally a new screen) to reopen as the Princes Film Theatre on Sunday with a two-week run of a rude French comedy, *The Green Mare's Nest*, inaugurating a foreign feature film policy in which it would compete with the Continentale, Kemp Town, for the latest releases, particularly those of a sensational nature. Late-night shows were introduced on Saturdays at 10.45 p.m. The Princes name was retained for only a few months: it became the Jacey Film Theatre from Sunday 25 September 1966.

In 1969, Brighton became one of only three places in the country to have its own full-time equivalent of London's National Film Theatre. This took over the Jacey Film Theatre which finished in typical style on Saturday 25 January with a week's run of 'Horror... Beyond Endurance!!', i.e. a tepid and trashy double bill of *The Flesh Eaters* plus *Death Curse of Tartu*, followed by a late-night dose of Hammer horrors, *The Reptile* plus *Plague of the Zombies*. The cinema was redecorated and reopened on Sunday 23 February 1969 as the Brighton Film Theatre (BFT) with a two-week run of the Swedish film *Elvira Madigan*, supported on the first evening by Sir Richard Attenborough in person introducing excerpts from *Oh! What a Lovely War*, which he had filmed in Brighton the previous year and which had yet to be released. The opening had been planned for 7 February, but was delayed by legal problems and the completion of redecoration.

The BFT offered two shows each evening with matinees on Wednesdays and at weekends and a late night presentation every Saturday. Some shows were open to members only, and many classic films were programmed, including *Berlin Olympiad* and *The Blue Angel*, plus a late-night season of Jean-Luc Godard films. Films could be shown on both 35mm and 16mm. There were 432 seats, retaining both stalls and balcony.

In fact, for the next year or so, the town was regaled with an extraordinary selection of films and personal appearances that made it a treasure trove of cinema unmatched before or since. Brighton's proximity to London enabled many stars and directors to travel down for personal appearances, along with others who already lived nearby. In just two months in 1969, you could have heard Flora Robson, Kenneth More, Sir John Clements, Dame Edith Evans and Jack Warner each introduce a major film in which they had appeared. And yet, to the shame of Brighton, the BFT lasted less than ten years.

The Odeon in West Street was modernised in the spring of 1969. The original tiles were replaced by ground stone in different colours and new tiles at street level. A modern canopy and a new name sign appeared, both lit from within. The name sign had none of the impact of neon but needed less maintenance. The above photograph (from the Cinema Theatre Association Archive) dates from *c.* 1972. The site next door, formerly occupied by the S.S. Brighton, has been cleared and awaits a much delayed redevelopment. (After Rank took over the S.S. Brighton, by then called the Palladium, in 1962, it was only allowed to demolish the building because it provided a replacement rink in the former Top Rank Suite, by this time the Top Rank Centre. However, this rink failed after a few years. The site of the S.S. Brighton became a temporary car park for twenty-five years until the Oak Hotel – Quality Hotel since 1999 – was built.)

The Odeon's auditorium was also altered at some point: the wooden dado survived but the splay walls were smoothed over, the grilles being replaced with plain versions over a much smaller opening (the Odeon clocks also disappeared). A new rectangular proscenium opening removed the curved top of the old one, and all the concealed lighting around the proscenium arch and across the ceiling went in favour of plain surfaces lit up from the balcony front. None of the alterations, inside or out, were an improvement.

six

The 1970s and 1980s

Attendances nationally continued their steady decline from 193 million in 1970 to a nadir of 54 million in 1984, improving to 94.5 million at the end of the decade. Some of this recovery was fuelled by new American-style multiplex cinemas, one of which was originally scheduled to open in 1989 at the Brighton Marina. In 1970, Brighton and Hove had ten cinemas. By 1980, it had seven containing twelve screens. Ten years later, it had eleven screens but these were contained within just three sites.

The 1970s saw the last years of the big auditoria. Faster release patterns saw a reduction in the number of films given the roadshow treatment. The Regent and ABC, Brighton, made use of their size to compete for closed-circuit TV relays of championship boxing matches by satellite in the early hours, including Muhammad Ali v. Joe Bugner from Las Vegas (15 February 1972), Joe Frazier v. George Foreman from Jamaica (23 January 1973) and George Foreman v. Muhammad Ali from Zaire (30 October 1974). The Odeon, West Street, offered live wrestling in 1971. One of the results of the shrinking audience was that even the ABC and the Odeon played soft porn films passed by the censor, often released by small distributors that would never have gained screen time in earlier years. The ABC ran *Emmanuelle* for five weeks in January-February 1975. The floodgates hadn't entirely opened: in 1986 Brighton Council saw fit to impose a ban on the Hollywood film *Nine ½ Weeks*. There was also an increasing tendency towards one-day presentations of more sophisticated material: films of Shakespeare, ballet, etc.

The large halls either closed or were subdivided. The worst decimation in the history of Brighton's cinemas occurred in less than three months during 1973 when all three of Rank's properties - the Odeon, the Regent and the Academy - closed as vacant space at the Top Rank Centre (rebranded Kingswest) was turned into a new three-screen Odeon.

The ABC was divided into four cinemas. With the new Odeon, it split the new films according to their ties with particular distributors. The Curzon (later Classic) then took the pick of the second run, leaving the Embassy and the Duke of York's to fight over the leftovers or show films on third run. As a sign of the changing times, the new Odeon staged its last Saturday morning children's show in early February 1979, when attendances had dropped to less than 100.

The 1980s brought a slow attrition of the remaining smaller cinemas. The Brighton Film Theatre made losses, gained subsidies, but closed in 1978, the building then becoming the home for a few years of the more commercially-minded Cinescene. The Curzon/Classic and the Vogue/Classic, the Embassy, Hove, and the Continentale, Kemp Town, all closed.

Only the Duke of York's survived as a single screen, reinventing itself as Brighton's home for specialised films. The one other positive development was the Odeon, Kingswest's investment in two additional cinemas in 1987 and one more in 1989, gearing itself up to compete with the forthcoming multiplex.

Buster Keaton Film Festival
PROGRAMME SUMMARY
Brighton Film Theatre, North Street

Brighton 29563
All seats bookable. Tickets 4/-, 6/- and 8/-.

JULY							
20	Mon		2.30	6.00	8.30	Our Hospitality	p.2
21	Tue		2.30	6.00	8.30	Battling Butler	p.3
22	Wed		2.30	6.00	8.30	Seven Chances	p.3
23	Thu		2.30	6.00	8.30	Go West	p.5
24	Fri		2.30	6.00	8.30	The General	p.5
25	Sat	2.00	4.00	6.00	8.30	Sherlock Jr.	p.6
26	Sun	2.00	4.00	6.00	8.30	Steamboat Bill Jr.	p.6
27	Mon		2.30	6.00	8.30	The Three Ages	p.7
28	Tue		2.30	6.00	8.30	College	p.8
29	Wed		2.30	6.00	8.30	The Navigator	p.8
30	Thu		2.30	6.00	8.30	Our Hospitality	p.2
31	Fri		2.30	6.00	8.30	Battling Butler	p.3
AUGUST							
1	Sat	2.00	4.00	6.00	8.30	Seven Chances	p.3
2	Sun	2.00	4.00	6.00	8.30	Go West	p.5
3	Mon		2.30	6.00	8.30	The General	p.5
4	Tue		2.30	6.00	8.30	Sherlock Jr.	p.6
5	Wed		2.30	6.00	8.30	Steamboat Bill Jr.	p.6
6	Thu		2.30	6.00	8.30	The Three Ages	p.7
7	Fri		2.30	6.00	8.30	College	p.8
8	Sat	2.00	4.00	6.00	8.30	The Navigator	p.8
9	Sun	2.00	4.00	6.00	8.30	Our Hospitality	p.2
10	Mon		2.30	6.00	8.30	Battling Butler	p.3
11	Tue		2.30	6.00	8.30	Seven Chances	p.3
12	Wed		2.30	6.00	8.30	Go West	p.5
13	Thu		2.30	6.00	8.30	The General	p.5
14	Fri		2.30	6.00	8.30	Sherlock Jr.	p.6
15	Sat	2.00	4.00	6.00	8.30	Steamboat Bill Jr.	p.6
16	Sun	2.00	4.00	6.00	8.30	The Three Ages	p.7
17	Mon		2.30	6.00	8.30	College	p.8
18	Tue		2.30	6.00	8.30	The Navigator	p.8
19	Wed		2.30	6.00	8.30	Our Hospitality	p.2
20	Thu		2.30	6.00	8.30	Battling Butler	p.3
21	Fri		2.30	6.00	8.30	Seven Chances	p.3
22	Sat	2.00	4.00	6.00	8.30	Go West	p.5
23	Sun	2.00	4.00	6.00	8.30	The General	p.5
24	Mon		2.30	6.00	8.30	Sherlock Jr.	p.6
25	Tue		2.30	6.00	8.30	Steamboat Bill Jr.	p.6
26	Wed		2.30	6.00	8.30	The Three Ages	p.7
27	Thu		2.30	6.00	8.30	College	p.8
28	Fri		2.30	6.00	8.30	The Navigator	p.8
29	Sat	2.00	4.00	6.00	8.30	Our Hospitality	p.2
30	Sun	2.00	4.00	6.00	8.30	Battling Butler	p.3

All films have piano accompaniment.
Printed by Kent Paper Company Ltd, London and Ashford, Kent.

BUSTER KEATON FILM FESTIVAL
BY SPECIAL ARRANGEMENT WITH LEOPOLD FRIEDMAN, TRUSTEE AND RAYMOND ROHAUER
BRIGHTON FILM THEATRE
20 JULY - 30 AUGUST 1970
OPEN TO THE PUBLIC

The Brighton Film Theatre brought the high standards of London's National Film Theatre to the south by such programming as a six-week season of ten Buster Keaton silent comedies with piano accompaniment in July/August 1970, and nine Mary Pickford silents in June 1971. There were foreign film revivals on Saturdays at 11 p.m. and some all-night shows of Kurosawa, etc. Most performances were open to the public, but members had their own days with special programming.

A remarkable event occurred on Friday 6 November 1970 at 11 p.m. when, just around the corner, the Regent had a gala screening of D.W. Griffith's silent epic *The Birth of a Nation* to assist the refurbishment of the Brighton Film Theatre. Despite heavy rain, crowds waited outside to see celebrities arrive by chauffeur-driven limousines from a champagne reception in the Royal Pavilion. They included Roger Moore, Michael Caine, Vincent Price (who introduced the film), Millicent Martin, Dora Bryan, Kay Hammond and husband Sir John Clements. The sum of £500 was raised for the BFT.

By the following year, however, the BFT had cut back on its bold repertory programming, mainly restricting classic films to members' shows on Sundays. It still maintained high standards with new foreign and specialised English-language films but with few of the special appearances and one-day events seen earlier.

By 1974, it was losing around £12,000 annually, with the British Film Institute meeting all but £1,000 of the deficit. The BFI decided to cap its subsidy to £7,000 annually and announced that the BFT would close unless the balance was made up locally. Attendances had slumped to less than half the 90,000 of its first year. An appeal was launched by Susannah York and Dame Flora Robson to raise £5,000. Brighton and East Sussex Councils joined donors in rescuing the BFT for the time being.

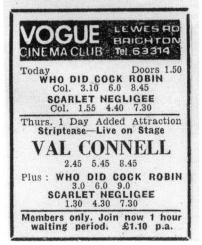

The Brighton Film Theatre in 1972 (courtesy of Cinema Theatre Association Archive) and the choice in adjacent press advertisements in January 1974 (see page 105 for details of the Vogue). The BFT carried on until Wednesday 13 December 1978 (the programme week ended on Wednesdays at all cinemas at this time). Its last three-day programme was a curious coupling of a minor 1961 gangster movie *Portrait of a Mobster* with the 1965 film of *Finnegan's Wake*. The Sunday before, the cinema had shown two classic Fritz Lang films, *You Only Live Once* and *Cloak and Dagger*. Its last foreign film was the previous Friday's late night showing of Ingmar Bergman's recent *Hour of the Wolf*. The lease (costing £4,000 per annum) was stated to expire on 25 December, and the British Film Institute declined to renew it for a further seven years, wanting a smaller auditorium seating 200-250 people with space for a club room, bar, information centre and bookshop.

A fourteen-year lease on the building on offer in March 1979 resulted in more than thirty expressions of interest. A return to cinema use was made more attractive by the impending closure of the Classic, Western Road. Miles Byrne, the current operator of the Embassy, Hove, and the Continentale, Kemp Town, reopened the former BFT as the Cinescene on Sunday 9 September 1979, the day after the Classic closed. It was billed as 'The Cinema In the Centre' and started off with the local premiere of the Merchant-Ivory film *The Europeans*.

The ABC, Hove, in its final years as a cinema. It underwent major alterations in 1970, closing on 3 December for the stalls area to become a 'luxury lounge' with high-backed seats in well-spaced rows, reopening with Disney's *The Aristocats* on Christmas Eve, concurrent with the Odeon, Brighton. Its seating capacity of 1,372 (already reduced from 1,592 in the 1950s) now came down to 1,016.

However, audiences did not respond favourably enough (some couldn't get used to the best seats being downstairs). When its owners, EMI, lodged an application for change of use to bingo in March 1974, a spokesman declared this merely a precautionary measure, but also indicated that it would not be a viable proposition to subdivide the existing cinema, and he rubbed it in by adding: 'Hove is just at the back of beyond cinematically'. Ladbroke's, the company which now ran the bingo at the former Essoldo in Brighton, successfully applied for a bingo licence for the ABC in May 1974. It closed on 5 June 1974. The film on the last night, *Callan*, drew less than fifty patrons.

After several years as part of Ladbroke's Lucky Seven bingo chain, it closed down, only to be reopened for bingo in late 1983 by the Lion Leisure Group. Lion was taken over by Granada, and so the building happened to regain its original name of Granada. After Granada's bingo halls were sold in May 1991, it became the Gala Club, soldiering on until 2003, when its closure in September was announced, to be followed by demolition for retirement homes. In mid-2003, the exterior looked shabby, even grim when approached from the flytower side, as white paint on the brickwork needed a new coat. The stalls area was in excellent decorative order, but some art deco friezes on the walls were the only signs of its 1930s decorative scheme, and the floor had been levelled off to continue onto the stage, with a false ceiling extending from the front of the balcony forwards, completely hiding the upper part of the building. Plain new grilles replaced (or concealed) the taller original ones seen in the above photograph (by John Fernee).

The Classic, former Curzon, Western Road, *c.* 1976 (courtesy of Chris Horlock), and auditorium on 2 March 1974 (photograph by John Fernee). The Curzon, Western Road, became part of the large Classic chain in the autumn of 1965, still picking up films after the ABC and Odeon. The interior was refurbished with 640 new seats and the cinema relaunched with a week of *Mary Poppins*. The Classic connection was increasingly emphasised in advertising until it was renamed the Classic from Sunday 18 July 1971. In November 1973, the company unveiled plans to subdivide the building into a casino and smaller cinema, but this never happened. It closed on Saturday 8 September 1979 following a week's run of *The Warriors*. The lease had eighteen months left but would not have been renewed, as the John Lewis Partnership had taken the site for a western extension of its Waitrose supermarket. Classic accepted a generous offer from John Lewis for the remainder of the lease.

The Classic, Lewes Road, in October 1980 (photograph by Allen Eyles). Shortly after taking over the Curzon, Western Road, the Classic chain acquired in March 1966 the small Randolph E. Richards circuit from the late founder's son, Julian D. (Douglas) Richards, obtaining some good first-run outlets in Eastbourne and Hastings. In the process, it also gained the Ace, Lewes Road, the former Gaiety (renamed from Sunday 21 November 1965) which still plodded along with films on their third or fourth Brighton run (only the Duke of York's got them later). The Ace was closed on Saturday 6 January 1968 after a three-day Disney revival of *Peter Pan* and *Westward Ho The Wagons!*, to be reopened by Classic as the Vogue Bingo and Social Club at the Ace on the following Thursday.

Then Classic sealed off the circle area to become the 336-seat Vogue Cinema from Thursday 22 January 1970, while bingo continued in the stalls. The cinema opened with *Easy Rider*, a film that had proved a smash hit for the Classic chain in London. However, the policy changed on Sunday 13 September 1970 when it became the first uncensored film club in Brighton with an annual membership fee of £1, restricted to those over eighteen. The initial presentation consisted of *The Wicked Die Slow* and *Professor Lust*, with daily matinees. The Vogue soon added a live stripper on Thursdays, and then on Tuesdays and Wednesdays as well. But, on Saturday 25 August 1979, two weeks before Classic gave up its Western Road outlet, the Vogue showed its last week of 'adult' films, *Sex Without Love* and *Can You Keep It Up for a Week?* An 11 p.m. show that same day of a new science-fiction film, *Star Crash*, reinstated mainstream public shows under the Classic name. However, the site was already under threat from a road improvement scheme. The Classic was forced to close on 31 October 1980. Demolition of the building, along with the adjoining shops and pub, was completed in August 1983. The cinema was remembered in the name of the new road layout: the Vogue Gyratory System.

Above: When the impending arrival of a new Odeon sealed the fate of the Academy, the Regent and the existing Odeon, the Academy was the first to go, with the appropriately titled *The Last Picture Show* on Wednesday 24 January 1973. The film had been scheduled for the preceding November, but delayed at the manager's request. Rank had intended to keep all three cinemas going until the new one was ready, but its opening had been delayed and the developers who had snapped up the Academy wouldn't wait. It was demolished almost immediately, to be replaced by a new Academy House. A large portion of one of the high side walls is said to have remained behind the building. In 2003, it stands opposite Regency Road, housing Yates's bar with offices above.

The Regent closed after a week of the musical *Cabaret* on Saturday 14 April (its ballroom had shut down on 30 June 1969). It was unusual in that its name had never been changed. All the other Regent cinemas built by PCT had been renamed Gaumont or Odeon. Most of it was demolished in 1974, the rest in 1977, to be replaced by the Boots store on an enlarged site. At one moment during 1977, an old poster for a 1920s film, *The White Dove*, was exposed to view. The vividly coloured ceramic panel, eight feet by three feet (seen top right), was saved and is seen on display at the Brighton Museum in 1984 (photograph courtesy of Chris Horlock). The design by C.J.L. Doman perhaps includes a suggestion of two film spools and strips of film unfurling (but there are tassels on the ends of the latter). One of the barrier ropes from the cinema hangs underneath. In 2003 the panel is mounted on the side wall of the film viewing area inside the Hove Museum. A plaque recalling the Regent has been placed by the Cinema Theatre Association in the Queen's Road entrance to Boots, which now occupies the site.

The Odeon was the last of the three Rank cinemas to shut, on Tuesday 17 April, with the Disney film *Snowball Express* and the cartoon *Saludos Amigos*. Despite being on a prime site, the building festered until 1990, being replaced by the Family Assurance office block in 1992.

Below: The first-floor entrance to the Odeon Film Centre was down the side of Kingswest from West Street (1973 photograph courtesy of Keith Skone).

The Rank Organisation opened its Top Rank Suite on the seafront at the corner of West Street and Kings Road in November 1965 as a dance hall with bars. It was immediately criticised as being an appalling eyesore on a highly-prominent site. An ice rink (doubling as a conference hall but too small for hockey matches) and fourteen-lane bowling alley were added in December 1966 when it became the Top Rank Centre. These replaced the ballroom at the Regent, the Top Rank Bowl at Hove, and the ice rink at the adjacent S.S. Brighton, which Rank demolished for an extension of the Top Rank Centre that never happened. The bowl closed in November 1970 and the ice rink also failed. The company then decided to spend over £1 million converting the vacant spaces into a three-screen Odeon Film Centre which had a gala opening on Wednesday 18 April 1973. The new Odeon had an inconspicuous first-floor entrance, reached by stairs and escalator, at the back of the site and its signs on the two street facades had to compete for attention with the other attractions. The complex was rebranded Kingswest at this time, combining the names of the two streets on which it stood. The three cinemas seated 390, 885 and 504 respectively – a total of 1,779. Odeon 1 opened with *Travels With My Aunt*, Odeon 2 with *The Poseidon Adventure* and Odeon 3 with *Alice's Adventures in Wonderland*. Odeons 1 and 2 were sometimes linked to show the same film and increase capacity. Odeons 1 and 3 had to be closed over the spring bank holiday weekend in 1974 for the floors at the rear to be strengthened. They reopened on 29 May with final repairs being carried out overnight. Odeon 3 could show 70mm prints and had extended runs over the next few years of films such as *Gandhi* and *Return of the Jedi*. All three auditoria were bland in design. The Odeon was obliged to advertise as part of Kingswest until the early 1990s.

ABC, Brighton, exterior in December 1983 (courtesy of Chris Horlock) and foyer in 1990 with stairs leading to ABC 1 in the old balcony (photograph by Ian Grundy). EMI, the ABC circuit's owner from 1969, has its logo in the last 'lozenge' on the vertical sign, replacing the triangle.

After the demise of the Regent, the ABC took to advertising as 'Brighton's Largest Cinema – 2,300 Seats'. However, its size no longer made economic sense, and it closed on Saturday 15 November 1975 to be split up into four cinemas. The last show in the single auditorium was the obscure *A Window to the Sky*, supported by the recent Charles Bronson western, *Valdez the Halfbreed*. When the building reopened on 3 April 1976, the largest cinema, ABC 1, seated 820 in the former balcony which had been extended forward with seven extra rows to a new proscenium arch that contained the old screen raised up. A new projection box was built at the back. ABCs 3 and 4, which seated 284 and 231 respectively, were created in the rear stalls, and divided by a passage which led to ABC 2, seating 346 in the former front stalls area and lower part of the stage, extending almost to the back wall. ABC 2 used the old projection room within the circle wedge, which was widened so that it could also project downwards into ABCs 3 and 4 onto mirrors which reflected the picture onto their screens. However, this proved unsatisfactory, and new boxes had to be built at the back of the two cinemas to provide direct projection.

ABC 1, the main auditorium (1990 photograph by Ian Grundy). A truncated ABC triangle seems to be set into the top of the new proscenium arch.

ABC 4 auditorium in April 1976, with the box attached to the ceiling containing the mirror used in projection. (Taken from the Chris Horlock collection.)

Opposite: The Embassy, Hove, in its final year (courtesy of Chris Horlock).
Above and below: The Embassy's auditorium (photographed by John Fernee).

The position of the Embassy'sscreen dates from 15 May 1950, following a month's closure, when the auditorium was extended by sixty feet onto vacant land. The seating capacity went up from 350 to 398, and the cinema changed name from Tivoli to Embassy. The flat side extension to the barrel-shaped ceiling reflects an old catwalk above. Until 2 November 1946, projectionists could only reach the box by climbing a ladder near the screen and crossing the roof. The cinema was closed after the box had been condemned as a fire hazard and couldn't reopen until Boxing Day 1946 after a new box, roughly four times larger, had been constructed with access from the front of the building.

In May 1979, the Embassy's proprietor, Miles Byrne, was refused permission to divide the building into a ground floor bingo hall and a new Brighton Film Theatre upstairs. The Embassy closed on Saturday 25 April 1981 following a week's run of a Disney programme, *The Spaceman and King Arthur* plus *Dumbo*. Still showing mainstream films late in the day, it had proved to be an amazing survivor. Its good location in a busy shopping and bedsit area had always helped, although it came to be regarded as a fleapit with rumours of rats in residence. From 1967 onwards it had been part of the Miles Byrne organisation, as passers-by were reminded by announcements on both the front and side wall. At one time, a panel down the side street displayed a map of Mr Byrne's handful of properties. These still included the tacky Continentale at Kemp Town and the recently opened CineScene.

The next owner of the Embassy turned it into the Black Cat bingo club. When that failed, it became the Pine Market, selling pine furniture. By May 1992 it had become Lazer Warriors ('The Ultimate Live Action Fantasy Game') and by December 1997, it was the arcade home of Nickelodeon Amusements. It was closed in mid-2003 with stiff opposition to plans to make it the Tivoli Club for lap dancing.

The Astoria shows its last attraction in 1977 (Chris Horlock collection). The long runs had continued, from *Paint Your Wagon* in 1970 and *Ryan's Daughter* in 1971 to *Murder on the Orient Express* in 1974 and *The Towering Inferno* in 1975. However, many top films had played at the ABC with its huge capacity, also on extended runs with separate performances, including *Love Story* in 1971 and *The Godfather* in 1972.

The Astoria had shown films in 3D, and 70mm prints on a giant screen. It had one last trick up its sleeve: the tremors of Sensurround accompanied *Earthquake* from Thursday 10 July to Wednesday 22 October 1975. Sensurround vibrated the air and created the illusion of the cinema shaking during the appropriate sequences of the film (audiences were assured that the building had been thoroughly surveyed to ensure their safety).

During the months that the ABC was being subdivided, the Astoria had the pick of the circuit's releases. But once the ABC reopened, it was relegated to a small afterthought in joint press advertising. It had become redundant and two months later, in June 1976, EMI gained a bingo licence.

However, it was almost a year before the Astoria showed its last film. In between such dross as a double bill of *Black Emmanuelle 2 Goes East* and *Fountain of Lust*, it had some choice offerings: Sensurround enhanced *Battle of Midway*, which ran for a month from mid-January 1977; and the final attraction was in 70mm, the Barbra Streisand version of *A Star Is Born*, which ran from 31 March to Saturday 7 May 1977. To the end, the Astoria maintained children's film shows on Saturday mornings.

EMI spent around £150,000, removing the huge screen and levelling the stalls floor for tables and new seating, before reopening the Astoria in June as a club for 1,000 bingo players. The original decorative scheme remained curtained over. The four-part vertical sign on the exterior gained a fifth 'lozenge' and spelt out the word BINGO. The relaunch as a bingo club forced the Duke of York's to drop its plans to reintroduce bingo on four nights a week from April 1977, which would almost certainly have led to full-time bingo or closure. Following changes of ownership, the Astoria became the Coral bingo club in the 1980s and a Gala club by 1992. It closed in 1997 when Gala moved to a new purpose-built bingo hall on Eastern Road.

On Friday 9 October 1981, the Duke of York's was relaunched as an art house by a new partnership of Pat Foster, Theo Simons and Gerald Hitman, setting it off on the course it has maintained ever since. Before they took over, it had staggered on with a mainstream revival policy, not opening until around 5.45pm on Saturdays and Sundays and around 7.15pm on weekdays(photograph courtesy of Hove Museum). On Saturday 12 September, it closed after a week's run of *The War of the Worlds* (a reissue of a 1953 feature) and a recent horror film, *The Sentinel*. Modest improvements were made during the month of closure before it reopened with a week's run of *The Aviator's Wife* followed by *Solaris* . In the spirit of the old Brighton Film Theatre, the Duke of York's also offered a Sunday afternoon double bill of *The Threepenny Opera* and the silent *Pandora's Box*, and a midweek revival of two Hitchcock classics, *Notorious* and *Rebecca*. There were around 460 seats, barely half the number in 1910. Club membership was a minor formality, added to the price of admission on a first visit.

The cinema could draw on the local student population from Brighton Poly and Sussex University, but its location away from the heart of town didn't help - except that it made the place less attractive for redevelopment or other uses. There were seasons of Japanese, Russian, Hitchcock, 'film noir', sci-fi and classic German films. Its biggest hits included *Fitzcarraldo* and *Diva*, and a one-day double bill of *Brighton Rock* and *The Third Man* which was repeated half a dozen times. Coffee, juices and cakes were sold instead of popcorn.

In mid-March 1983, the cinema was put on the market as a going concern. It closed on Tuesday 7 June 1983 following a world premiere run of the British film *The Ploughman's Lunch*, having been taken over by William Heine, who ran two art houses in Oxford. There was some delay in completing the takeover and a row broke out over vandalism which occurred while it was dark, including an unofficial concert staged by punk rockers on Saturday 23 July. In any event, Mr Heine reopened the Duke of York's on Thursday 4 August 1983. Its seating capacity was now reduced to 302 and a new sound system had been installed. The very first show, a matinee of the musical *Annie*, was cancelled after no one showed up, but a 4.30pm performance of *Frances* and the 7pm and 9pm screenings of Fassbinder's controversial *Querelle* had more success. Little money seems to have been spent (perhaps little was available) and the cinema became endearingly shabby (except that its toilet facilities were beyond the pale).

Above: The Cinescene, North Street, in May 1985. *Below:* The Continentale, Kemp Town, in September 1983, tempting a couple to see its sex double bill of *Eager Fingers Eager Lips* and *Hot Lunch*. (Both pictures from the Chris Horlock collection.)

The long run of cinema in North Street came to an end when Miles Byrne closed the Cinescene on Saturday 23 June 1983 following a week of *Gandhi*. Although it had played art house fare like the black comedy *Eating Raoul*, it had lost ground to the Duke of York's and there was adverse publicity when an ornamental grille fell from the ceiling into the auditorium, shutting it for five days until 11 May 1981. For some time there had been only one evening performance except at weekends when shows started at 5.40pm. It then stood disused until March 1988 when work started on its conversion into a Burger King restaurant. This took up the former entrance and the adjacent shop, and the area under the balcony. For many years the front stalls became an overflow or party area, with the original screen, curtains, ceiling and balcony all visible, along an old advertising board from its news theatre days on the balcony front. The balcony was used for storage. In the early 1990s, a video projector was installed and local film-makers showed their work on the screen. In a 1998 refit, the old cinema trappings were removed (the advertising panel went for display at the Hove Museum). A new ceiling extended forwards from the underside of the balcony, the stage was converted to a children's area, and the only hint of the old auditorium was the sloping floor. Burger King renewed the cinema theme with a dado in the design of a film strip with sprocket holes, posters on the walls, statues of Bogart, Chaplin and Monroe, and a new screen for the video projector. However, a huge, colourful mural of film stars on the upper part of the facade had to be removed because it lacked planning permission and was deemed to be in poor taste.

Mr Byrne was left with the Continentale, Kemp Town, which carried on until his death. Like the Vogue, it became a club offering uncensored sex films with titles like *Bikiniless Capers*. The last press advertising to be traced extends to 1 January 1987. It has now been converted to flats.

The sixth mini-screen on the ground floor of the Odeon at Kingswest (Chris Horlock collection).

On Thursday 21 May 1987, the Odeon added two more cinemas and switched to a ground floor entrance and foyer which were linked to a new arcade leading to the seafront. The outside stairs and escalator to the old foyer were demolished, making more space for the new hotel that was built next door in the early 1990s. With 275 and 242 seats respectively, the new cinemas occupied a former fun pub and roller skating rink, and shared a ground floor entrance off the new foyer, one being on that floor and the other directly underneath, reached by a staircase. Both were wide and low-ceilinged with a decent screen size (the upper one could show 70mm prints). The seating capacity was now 2,284 in five screens. The Odeon plunged into an experimental film promotion called Cinema 87 which arranged thirty advance screenings of new mainstream pictures between 21 and 25 May 1987 there and at the Cannon (former ABC).

When work was underway on the out-of-town multiplex cinema, the Odeon further geared itself up for the challenge by opening a sixth screen in August 1989: this was on the ground floor and out on a limb, shoehorned into disused kitchen space and entered to the left of the screen. It seated 103, with its own projection box, and has been designated as a 'mini cinema'.

The ABC has become the Cannon after the ABC circuit passed to the Cannon Group (photograph by Allen Eyles). The name change took effect on Thursday 18 December 1986. *Below.* In April 1988 the Odeon is part of Kingswest Boulevard advertising. Note that both cinemas offer separate performances and indefinite runs, with no smoking and bargain prices for early evening shows.

All the fun, rolled into one!

KINGSWEST BOULEVARD

ON THE SEAFRONT OPEN FROM 12 noon daily

TopRankSuite.
732627
Tonight
Saturday Night Out
Special appearance by outrageous dance duo "Hot Flesh"
9-2. Smart dress. Over 18's only.
This ad. admits 2 for only £2 each B4 10.30 p.m. on Sat. 16/4/88
Mon. 18th April — Johnny Clegg

Boulevard
PASTA PIZZA RESTAURANT
3-course traditional Sunday lunch
£4.95
Bookings 25897

Busby's
Tel. 25899
9 p.m. — 2 a.m.
KEEP THIS FREQUENCY CLEAR!
Due to atmospheric conditions we will be experiencing great excitement and a Full House — Come Early!

First Choice **ODEON** BRIGHTON 25890 LICENSED BAR

RETAINED! RICHARD DREYFUSS **STAKEOUT** (15) Sep. perf. 1.20 3.40 6.00B 8.20 Sat. & Sun. 6.00 & 8.20 only Bargain show 6.00 Mon./Sat.	RETAINED! WILLIAM HURT ALBERT BROOKS HOLLY HUNTER **BROADCAST NEWS** (15) Sep. perf. 2.00 5.20B 8.10 Bargain show 5.20 Mon./Sat.	RETAINED! JOHN LONE JOAN CHEN PETER O'TOOLE YING RUOCHENG **THE LAST EMPEROR** (15) Two sep. perfs. 2.15 & 7.15 Feature 2.30 and 7.30
JOHN HUSTON'S **THE DEAD** (U) ANGELICA HUSTON DONA McCANN Four sep. progs. 2.00 4.15 6.30B 8.45 Bargain show 6.30 Mon./Sat.	RETAINED! They exist, fear them **THE BELIEVERS** (18) Starring Martin Sheen 1.20 3.40 6.00B 8.20 Bargain show 6.00 Mon./Sat.	Special Matinees Saturday & Sunday at 1.45 & 4.00 WALT DISNEY'S **THE FOX AND THE HOUND** Children £1.75 (U)

Please note: All auditoria designated non-smoking

CANNON FILM CENTRE EAST STREET BRIGHTON TEL: 27010

NOW SHOWING Cher & Nicholas Cage **MOONSTRUCK** (PG) Four sep. perfs. daily at 1.10 3.35 6.00(T) and 8.20 NO SMOKING	NOW SHOWING Steven Spielbergs film of **EMPIRE OF THE SUN** (PG) Two sep. progs. daily at 2.00 and 7.25 NO SMOKING	NOW SHOWING Charles Bronson **DEATH WISH 4 The Crackdown** (18) Four sep. progs. daily at 1.10 3.25 5.45(T) and 8.20 NO SMOKING	NOW SHOWING Michael Douglas Glenn Close **FATAL ATTRACTION** (18) Three sep. progs. daily at 2.10 5.00(T) and 8.00 NO SMOKING

TWILIGHT PERFORMANCES (T) Monday to Saturday ALL SEATS £1.50
Tickets may be obtained from 1.30 to 6.30 pm on 202095 with Visa/Access details

Cinema has made a dramatic comeback, attendances nationally rising from 97 million in 1990 to 176 million in 2002, mainly as a result of the proliferation of American-style multiplex cinemas which appealed to teenagers as a break with the past. The new Metro-Goldwyn-Mayer Cinemas brought the multiplex revolution to Brighton Marina, leaving the Odeon and Cannon to continue as city centre alternatives. The Cannon regained its old name of ABC under new ownership but closed in 2000, after which the Odeon spruced itself up to multiplex standards with the same number of screens as its Marina Village rival.

On 28 April 1995, new cinema facilities were opened by Lord Attenborough at the Gardner Arts Centre on the campus of the University of Sussex at Falmer. There was a special showing of Attenborough's film version of *Oh! What a Lovely War* on a 22ft wide screen. Dolby stereo sound was installed and there were 350 seats. Films continue to be shown there part of the time. As part of national celebrations of the Centenary of Cinema, on 25 March 1996 plaques were unveiled not only at the seafront location of the first film show in Brighton, but also at the Duke of York's, where a touring live presentation, 'The Living Picture Show', had its first production. The same day was used to launch the new sixty-six-seat Brighton Media Centre in Middle Street, where specialised films are still shown in 2003 on several nights of the week.

Changes in the bingo industry threatened two former cinema buildings. Following a takeover of the Mecca company, Rank decided to keep Mecca's club in the listed Hippodrome Theatre and close its Top Rank Club in the former Essoldo in North Street, even though this had been fully refurbished in 1987. In 1995, Rank spent £3.5 million converting the latter into a leisure complex, featuring a Hotshots night club, a New Orleans-style Jumpin' Jaks bar in the balcony, and a bowling alley in the stage area. Despite considerable structural additions, many of the theatre trappings, including the proscenium arch and side boxes, remained. The complex closed two years later. Rank had completed a hat-trick of failure with unhappy consequences for the area, following its bowl at Hove (for which the Odeon was closed) and its Top Rank Centre (which brought about the demise of the Academy, the Odeon and the Regent). The alterations inside the North Street building made a return to theatrical use punitively expensive; but the town needed a large venue for touring shows, a leading entrepreneur expressed interest, and there was considerable dismay when the building was demolished for large shopping units.

Film showings began springing up in unusual places. The new owners of the Duke of York's hosted a free showing of *Jurassic Park* in Preston Park on a giant screen held up by a crane. In August 1996 'Stella Artois Movie Classics' put on free late-evening screenings of *Jaws* and *Some Like It Hot* on a sixty foot by twenty foot screen set across Brighton beach between the piers. This continued, with 'Stella Artois On Location' presenting *Moulin Rouge* and *Quadrophenia*, the Brighton-set story of teenage gang battles, in July 2002.

The singalong version of *The Sound of Music* arrived on Wednesday 23 February 2000 at the Theatre Royal in Brighton: 'The classic film musical - now with subtitles - so everyone can join in! Take your vows, tear down those drapes and hurry to catch London's sell-out sensation. Join in all the numbers, boo the Nazis, hiss the Baroness and attend the ultimate karaoke event of the century'. It has made several return visits.

Brighton is fortunate to have the Duke of York's as a fine example of the early cinema, and it looks as though one of its 1930s cinemas may be restored to something like its original form and possibly show the occasional film.

In 1999, the leaseholders of the former Astoria, Bass Leisure, were refused a drinks licence to turn it into a young people's theme pub called It's a Scream. The Astoria Moving

Picture Trust was formed by cinema enthusiasts Colin Dibley and Matthew May, along with Brighton architect Nimrod Ping, in the hope of restoring the building to a single large-screen cinema showing classic films interspersed with live shows.

A development company planned to replace it with flats - until it became a Grade II listed building on 22 November 2000 as a result of representations by the Astoria Moving Picture Trust. A detailed inspection by English Heritage revealed that 'its decoration survives remarkably intact under later alterations, and includes in the proscenium frieze work of unusual quality.' The listing notice concludes: 'It is particularly unusual in its French art deco style, of which it is a rare cinematic survivor. This style was adopted by [architect Edward A.] Stone for his Whitehall Theatre, City of Westminster (grade II), and can be seen in other West-End theatres, notably the Cambridge; but this is a larger and more elaborate example intended to demonstrate that a South Coast ciné-variety hall could match the West End in sophistication.'

In August 2001, the Brighton-based company of the performing group Stomp, Yes/No Productions, acquired the Astoria for £900,000 from the developer. It has appointed an architect to restore the building, and the result is awaited with optimism.

The cinemagoing scene seems to have stabilised. Back in the autumn of 1997, Virgin signed up with developer Citygrove Leisure to operate a new multiplex in Hove as part of a £30 million redevelopment of the Council-owned King Alfred Leisure Centre. By the winter of 1998, this had become a £10 million cinema with thirteen screens and 3,414 seats. In response to fears over increased traffic, the cinema was scaled back to 2,000-2,500 seats. Planning permission was granted in September 1999 for a scheme including eleven cinemas, and then rescinded following objections. In 2003 the Council favoured a new scheme for a sports centre with four tower blocks of flats and no cinemas.

Another multiplex is possible when and if there is a massive redevelopment of the area the east of Brighton Station. The £500 million scheme announced in July 1997 by London & Amsterdam Properties proposed a twelve-screen multiplex cinema.

The original art deco floor pattern in the foyer and decorative grillework in the auditorium of the Astoria are shown to survive in these photographs taken by the Astoria Moving Picture Trust in 2000.

Above: The readagraph on the seafront façade of the Cannon Cinema promotes the forthcoming multiplex in the Marina Village (1991 photograph by Allen Eyles).

Being under the same ownership as the Metro-Goldwyn-Mayer multiplex, the Cannon would normally have been closed to concentrate attendances on the new site. In fact, the Cannon was put up for sale in April 1991 but remained open for the time being as it still did moderately well and took away many of the top releases from the Odeon. However, the 820-seat upstairs auditorium was shut in May 1991, leaving only the three lower screens (which now seated 345, 271 and 194, a total of 810). Subsequently, the cinema seems to have been taken off the market. By 1994, it was offering cut-price admission to all but the last evening show. It was certainly clean and well-run, but also run-down and sad. After Virgin acquired the Cannon-MGM circuit, it quickly sold most of the older cinemas to a new ABC Cinemas company which returned the ABC name on 14 June 1996 and even revived the old triangle logo, while continuing to promote low prices.

The cinema was later put up for sale and just squeezed into the new millennium by closing on 20 January 2000. The interior has been gutted and the East Street entrance now serves a pub called Toad at The Picture House, with a completely new decor and rearrangement of part of the ground floor that retains no cinema details. The seafront entrance is used by the Grosvenor Casino which occupies upstairs space that again removes all traces of the old cinema. At least the exterior has been nicely cleaned up.

Below: The Marina was first seriously planned in the 1960s to bring a harbour to Brighton. It opened to the public in July 1979, purely as a harbour for boats, and was taken over in 1985 by developer Brent Walker. This company added a supermarket, houses, flats and shops to create a marina village. The development also suited a multiplex cinema with its out-of-town location and plentiful parking space. American Multi-Cinema (AMC), which opened this country's first multiplex with ten screens at Milton Keynes in November 1985, signed a deal with Brent Walker for a ten-screen cinema at the Marina. The location of the multiplex was moved to below a multi-storey car park in early 1987. AMC anticipated opening around Christmas 1989. Then Cineplex Odeon (a Canadian company using the name Gallery Cinemas) took over the scheme in March 1988, planning to open in mid-1990, but sold out to the Cannon circuit, which operated the former ABC in Brighton. By the time the multiplex was nearing completion, Cannon was part of the French-owned Pathé Communications empire, which included the famous American studio Metro-Goldwyn-Mayer (MGM). This allowed the Metro-Goldwyn-Mayer name and logo of the roaring lion to be applied to the multiplex when it finally opened with eight screens, all with Dolby stereo, on Friday 3 May 1991. Free previews were shown in six auditoria on the preceding day. As the advertisement shows, nine different films were initially offered.

1991 view of the multiplex's entrance (from Cinema Theatre Association Archive, donated by Jack Lawrence). The structure over the pavement has since been removed.

The Metro-Goldwyn-Mayer Cinemas had an unprepossessing exterior, quite unworthy of their illustrious name. They occupied the base of an unsightly and long unused multi-storey car park, only too visible as one descended into the Marina. The front entrance faced a road with hoardings on the other side, behind which a square and a hotel were promised at a later date. Cinemagoers used the large ground-level car park at the back of the cinema, which also served the supermarket as well as the shops, restaurants and bars at the Marina. To reach the cinema entrance, patrons had to walk through an enclosed passage down one side of the cinema and turn right. At one time, illuminated poster displays were placed around the start of the passage, which was brightly lit and even had soft music (The unused car park on top of the cinema became a dumping ground for tyres, adding to its unsightliness as viewed on entering the Marina.)

Two pay boxes were set in the cinema's outer foyer, after which a few steps led up to a wide main foyer with a rectangular ceiling recess unimaginatively covered in ceiling tiles. A concessions counter was placed across the back wall, with doors on each side leading to four matching auditoria, seating 351, 251, 223, then 202 and 203 in the smallest pair (why the one-seat difference is not known). This provided a total seating capacity of 2,055 in the eight auditoria, roughly comparable to the former Regent or Odeon, West Street, with a single screen. With eight screens, it played all the best new films at the same time as the Odeon and Cannon in the town centre. By August 1995, the Metro-Goldwyn-Mayer name had been abbreviated to a more manageable MGM.

Left: This May 1991 photograph shows one of the Metro-Goldwyn-Mayer Cinemas' auditoria with the festoon curtain raised. The two rear rows of the central block in all the screens were left clear, behind the rails seen at the back, for wheelchair users. The curtains have been permanently raised in recent years. (Courtesy of Chris Horlock.)

The auditoria were the best feature of the Metro-Goldwyn-Mayer multiplex. Spacious with solid plaster ceilings (rather than cheap ceiling tiles), they made an attractive impression with festoon curtains, the upper half of the side and rear walls covered in red drapes and lit from below, and comfortable red seats with adequate legroom. There was a conventional rake to the single floor of each auditorium, so that heads in front could still spoil the view of the screen (the later generation of multiplexes has adopted stepped or stadium seating to overcome this problem).

Below: a giant screen across Brighton beach for 'Stella Artois Movie Classics' in August 1996 (photograph by Allen Eyles).

Above: The Brighton film scene in October 1998. The Cannon-MGM circuit has been acquired by Virgin, which rebranded the MGM multiplexes with its own name - in Brighton, from 28 June 1996 - and sold older properties including the Cannon to a new ABC company that returned the old ABC name and triangle logo to the building and competed for patrons with low prices. The Odeon has escaped from advertising as part of Kingswest. Children's shows are advertised at the Virgin and Duke of York's.

In January 1997, Virgin sought planning permission to add ten screens across the road from its entrance, to be connected by a bridge. This would have provided the biggest cinema on the South Coast. However, Virgin sold its British cinemas to a major French operator, Union Générale Cinématographique, which rebranded all the sites with its unattractive initials, including Brighton from Friday 17 March 2000. UGC appears to have shown no interest in enlarging Brighton or proceeding with Virgin's Hove multiplex scheme.

In early 2003, the UGC multiplex in Brighton Marina was in need of major refurbishment. Its drab frontage, featuring a patchy selection of framed quad posters, is now fully exposed to view by the wide but barren Park Square in front. Nothing much seems to have changed inside. The festoon curtains have been disused since Virgin days in favour of continuous slides before the film programme starts. The carpet and seats seem to be the originals. The ceilings have been painted dark blue.

Below: The Duke of York's portico has 20ft-long cancan dancer's legs protruding in September 1994, just after it had been repainted by new owners (photograph by Allen Eyles). The previous lessee, William Heine, was a devotee of outlandish fibreglass sculptures. He commissioned these legs for a cinema he had renamed Not the Moulin Rouge at Headington, Oxford. When this closed, Mr Heine transferred the legs to Brighton in 1991. He also gave the Duke of York's some of the Oxford cinema's pedestal seats with purple upholstery decorated with heart shapes. These mingled with at least two other types of dilapidated cinema seating.

The Duke of York's passed into the hands of receivers in August 1994. It seems to have been trading profitably, as it was kept open to be sold as a going concern. Several bids were received, and the cinema was taken over on 14 October 1994 by City Screen, an expanding art house chain with a high reputation. The crisis seems to have prompted the Grade II listing of the building on 24 November 1994.

Although the cancan dancer's legs were not mentioned in the listing description and could have been scrapped, City Screen astutely realised what a talking point they had become. A crane was brought in to elevate the sculpture to a more prominent position at the top of the façade, allowing the balcony to be opened up as an extension of a new licensed bar. The legs are also used in the background of the advertisement on the facing page.

Virgin CINEMAS

Brighton Marina

a14329

Programmes From Friday 16th October

Saving Private Ryan 15
1.15 5.05 8.45

Mulan U
12.40 3.05 5.30 8.00

A Perfect Murder 15
1.10 3.50 6.30 9.10
Late Show Saturday 12.00

Lock Stock And Two Smoking Barrels 18
*Not Saturday & Sunday
*1.10 *4.00 6.40 9.30

Ever After PG
12.20 3.20 6.20

Godzilla PG
Saturday & Sunday Only
12.00 2.55

Halloween H20 18
Friday Evening 10.25
Saturday Evening 10.25 12.30

The Truman Show PG
1.30 4.10 7.00 9.40
Late Show Saturday 12.15

There's Something About Mary 15
1.40 5.35 8.30 9.20
Late Show Saturday 11.20
See "There's Something About Mary" and win FREE Virgin Atlantic Flights for life.

Lethal Weapon 4 15
*Not Saturday & Sunday
*2.10 6.05 9.00

Doctor Dolittle PG
Saturday & Sunday only 1.00 3.40

CHILDREN'S SATURDAY MORNING CINEMA
Grease PG
Saturday 17th October
All seats £1.50
Doors Open 10.00
Programme ends 12.30

All programmes subject to late change
Adult discount prices before 5pm daily

Free parking. Air conditioning throughout.

24 hour programme information and credit card booking:
0541 555 145

Virgin CINEMAS

ODEON

a33728

DISCOUNT SEAT PRICES BEFORE 7PM EVERY DAY OF THE WEEK

ODEON FILM LINE 0870 50 50 007
24hr advance booking and information service
Visit our Website at:
www.odeon.co.uk

CAMERON DIAZ MATT DILLON
there's something about mary

This film is crude, rude & hilarious
12.50 3.10 5.40 8.15 (15)

LOCK STOCK AND TWO SMOKING BARRELS (18)
Featuring VINNIE JONES & STING
1.15 3.35 6.00 8.30
From Tomorrow 6.15 8.35

MICHAEL DOUGLAS
GWYNETH PALTROW
A Perfect Murder
1.15 3.30 6.00 8.20 (15)

Walt Disney's
MULAN (U)
Fri & Sat 1.00 3.15 5.30 7.45
Sun - Thurs 1.30 3.50 6.10 8.20

EVER AFTER
This Year's Romeo & Juliet
1.40 5.10 8.00 (PG)
From Friday 1.00 3.40

Wednesday 21st October
ROBERT DUVALL
FARRAH FAWCETT
The Apostle (12)
1.45 5.05 8.00

A Steven Spielberg Film
TOM HANKS EDWARD BURNS
MATT DAMON TOM SIZEMORE

saving private ryan
12.55 4.10 7.35 (15)

JIM CARREY
the **TRUMAN** show
1.00 3.30 5.55 8.20 (PG)

Special Screening
Friday and Saturday night at 9.50pm
HALLOWEEN: H20
(18)

Discount parking in NCPs Churchill 2 car park for £1.85 from 5.15pm - Collect your discount voucher when you purchase your ticket

ABC

BRIGHTON
INFO 01273 327010
BOOKING FROM 1PM DAILY
VISA · M'CARD · NO BOOKING FEE
01273 202095

a8843

Last day
SAVING PRIVATE RYAN (15)
7.30 only

THE TRUMAN SHOW (PG)
1.40 3.55 6.15 8.35

THERE'S SOMETHING ABOUT MARY (15)
1.45 5.45 8.20

MULAN (U)
from Friday
1.35 3.40 5.50 8.15

WWW.ABCCINEMAS.CO.UK
ALL SEATS BEFORE 7PM £2.50 · AFTER 7PM ADULTS £3.00

DUKE OF YORK'S
PREMIER PICTURE HOUSE
Box Office (01273) 602503
24 Hr Prog Info (01273) 626261
www.picturehouse-cinemas.co.uk

Portrait of Francis Bacon
LOVE IS THE DEVIL
(18)
Today: 2.00, 5.45

Steve Martin in
THE SPANISH PRISONER
(PG)
Today: 4.15, 8.45

FROM FRIDAY:
MEN WITH GUNS (15)
BUFFALO 66 (15)
POINT BLANK (15)

Junior Dukes
MR MAGOO (PG)

Before the film starts, why not unwind and enjoy a relaxing drink in our Balcony Bar

Opposite: After City Screen took over, it soon closed the Duke of York's for two weeks for repairs and redecoration, relaunching it on Friday 3 March 1995 with *Bandit Queen*, and complimentary drinks for patrons at the 6.15 performance. The listing scotched plans to install a larger screen and improve the rake of the stalls floor. When various improvements were completed in October 1997, the Duke's was looking better, inside and out, than at any time since the 1920s, with much-needed new gents' toilet facilities in the basement. The proscenium arch seen at right, with its raised star pattern lit by concealed lighting, was the one installed for CinemaScope in 1955. The curtains have been opened up to show the full width of the screen (March 2000 photograph by Allen Eyles).

Welcome as the changes were, there had been something very endearing about the Duke of York's before it was smartened up. Its scruffiness and its imaginative programming made its mainly student clientele feel at home, and the projection was usually fine. Its publicity programmes had been collectable: large folded sheets opening out into a poster on one side with detailed descriptions of the films on the back. The Duke of York's now became a public cinema, and its monthly programme had a more conventional size and appearance, but its choice of films remained almost as adventurous as before.

Although a single-screen cinema was by now an anachronism, City Screen had no plan to subdivide the auditorium (listed building consent might have been obtained for 'reversible' changes) but it was concerned to maximise the important subsidiary income from food and drink. The Duke of York's tiny foyer was extended into the back of the stalls with a new wall that took in the four columns supporting the balcony. This allowed a new refreshments counter to be set up. Similarly, a licensed bar was established upstairs by extending the back wall of the balcony foyer into the auditorium, losing more seats but retaining what was left of the opened-up box at the back right hand side. The seats in the stalls have all been replaced by one uniform type discarded by a High Wycombe multiplex and since reupholstered in blue. The total number of seats became 327.

The Duke of York's remains the cinematic gem of Brighton and the oldest cinema in the entire country still retaining most of its original appearance. Remarkably, it has never changed its name and never been anything but a cinema. 'This is an enriching building which stands out as an island of beauty in an otherwise barren part of Brighton,' declared Dr Anthony Seldon in his book, *Brave New City* (2002).

The Duke of York's has shown a flair for publicity. On Saturday 16 September 2002, it screened a specially made 90-second film in which a patron proposed to his girlfriend while both were seated in the audience (the lady said yes). A week later, it showed six shorts made digitally by Brighton producers to a full house.

The owners have been anxious to expand. A single screen is very costly to operate. It limits programming, and the Duke of York's is said to be barely making a profit. In April 2002, it was proposed to add two new 120-seat cinemas plus a preview cinema over the adjacent fire station to plans prepared by architect Simon Huspeth. This would have also provided additional space for the ground floor foyer and upstairs bar. Local residents and firemen fiercely opposed the scheme. Since then, there has been an unsuccessful bid to build two additional cinemas in place of a chapel to the other side of the fire station on Viaduct Road.

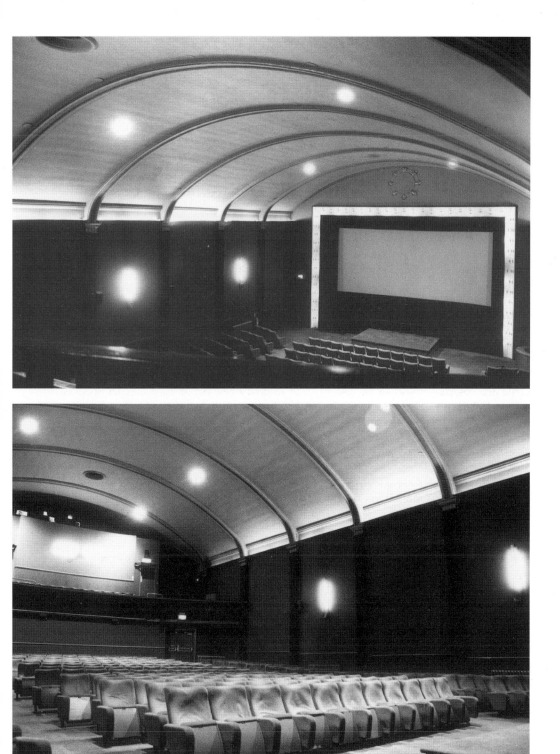

Boasting a revised style of logo, the Odeon still competes with other Kingswest attractions for attention in this August 2003 photograph (by Allen Eyles). In May 1999 hopes were raised that Kingswest might be demolished in favour of a new leisure development to include an Odeon multiplex costing £10 million, with ten screens seating 2,550. The ground floor would have housed bars and restaurants, including a Hard Rock Café. A revised scheme in October promised not only the ten Odeon screens (totalling 2,590 seats with one 500-seat auditorium doubling as a conference centre) but also three restaurants, a casino and a new club. Rank was anxious to get going before a new multiplex could be built at Hove, and demolition could have started within six months. However, according to an Odeon source, the proposal was scuppered when the landlord, a major insurance company which bought Kingswest from Brighton Council *c.* 1996, would not give its consent.

A decision was taken to upgrade the existing building at a cost of £2 million, subdividing the largest Odeon auditorium into three screens which opened on Friday 14 December 2001 in time for part one of the *Lord of the Rings* trilogy (shown on three screens with staggered starting times). The new auditoria were fully up to modern multiplex standards with stadium seating in widely spaced rows and curtains in front of the screen. The other five cinemas remained open during the three months of refurbishment, and there was an overall reduction of only 100 seats. Dolby digital surround sound was provided in five auditoria. The external approach remains unfriendly, the internal layout awkward, but the new-look foyer and passages, using predominantly dark blue with areas in green and orange, are welcoming. The Odeon's eight screens put it on a par with the multiplex at the Marina, but with a higher total seating capacity of 2,217 (389 + 220 + 238 + 238 + 514 + 286 + 232 + 100).